Follow
the
Yarn

D1569453

ADVANCE PRAISE FOR
Follow the Yarn

The doing and the daring are the magic keys to unlocking the treasure chest.
— from *Follow the Yarn*

Follow the Yarn is a triple threat! First, it is a superb study guide for anyone who knits or ever wanted to knit; second, it is a deeply moving story of a mentor and her student; and finally, it is an inspiring tale of the author finding her voice as a writer. Reba's clear, luminous style smoothly combines Ann Sokolowski's encyclopedic knowledge of knitting with lively, humorous anecdotes. *Follow the Yarn* is a fitting tribute to a master teacher and a one-of kind-woman.
— Gail Straub, co-founder, Empowerment Institute;
author, *Returning to My Mother's House: Taking Back the Wisdom of the Feminine*

There is so much wisdom in this book. *Follow the Yarn* is about being mindful to what you hear, feel, and smell, and the surprises that arise when you commit to being awakened by life. Read to learn about knitting, and about your Self.
— Rabbi TZiPi Radonsky, coach; author,
And: Building a World of Connection Through Jewish Mystical Wisdom

Follow the Yarn is not your typical knitting book. It is a heartfelt journey of empowerment and a loving testament to the generosity, wit, and wisdom of a gifted teacher. It is also chock full of knitting tips, techniques, and Ann Sokolowski's standards of excellence. Each knitting lesson provides rich metaphors and life lessons: "Don't leave loose ends," "Know which mistakes to tear out and which ones to let lie." The author shares the gifts of her teacher, Ann, and she also shares the gift of her heart, wide open. Instruction, inspiration, and love — all in one delightful package.
— Marcy Nelson-Garrison, creator, CoachingToys and The PINK Paradigm

The story of how one person can inspire, teach, and empower others, while sitting at a table and making loops in string. The reader will find tips and tricks, stitch samplers, beginning and finishing methods and techniques, as well as a chronicle of relationships forged with fiber and sticks.
— Becky Yoder, blogger, Sunnybrook Yarns

If you like reading autobiographies and enjoy knitting, you'll enjoy this book. After reading it, I have more confidence to go out and just knit something, independent of a pattern. I'll definitely be keeping this one on file, and coming back to it in the future.
— Jane Galley, blogger, Loopy's Place

It's not just about knitting, it's about the stitches that bind together the important parts of our lives.
— Gene Krackehl, author, *You Are the Healer*

What started as a project to tell Ann's story became a means to allow the author to work through some long-standing issues of her own. Sometimes painfully raw, you can see the hurt and the healing happening. By the end of the book, you have a sense that you know Ann, a gruff New Yorker with a heart of gold. Finally, there is a great sense of peace, and you just know that your knitting is going to get better.
— Alison Manning, blogger, Tales From An Old Stone House

Poignant and poetic, heartfelt and funny, Linker knits a neat story of life, learning, and love. Readers will eagerly follow her yarn, and gain greater understanding of the stitches they use to create the fabric of their own lives.
— Laurie Graff, author, *You Have to Kiss a Lot of Frogs* and *The Shiksa Syndrome*

Who would think that great wisdom could be passed on by teaching and learning knitting? Not for knitting lovers only, this is a how-to-knit book, yes, but more importantly a story of healing and inspiring wisdom. Reba Linker knits these two threads craftily, creating an easy, worthwhile read.
— Marilyn Graman, co-founder, Lifeworks;
co-author, *There is No Prince, How to Be Cherished,* and *The Female Power Within*

Your attachment to Ann says everything. This is Ann. The way you wrote it is exactly how we feel. Some people might be intimidated by Ann. She was not for everyone. She could be brutally honest, but I like that — it's hard to get someone to be that honest in today's world. And it's not just me; all of us at the store felt the same way, all of us understood her.
— Raymond Stambouli, manager, Smiley's Yarns

Grace has been knitted into every little fabric of the book — how powerful it is. Thank you so much, Reba Linker, for your powerful share.
— Sharon McWilliams, The Gift Life Coach, Wise WomanSoul

Simply brilliant! The yarn gives people a foundation, a building block on which to begin their story. What a gift you are sending out into the world!
— Judy Ranieri, coach; creator, The Wisdom Box and The Notebook Project

Follow the Yarn

The Knitting Wit & Wisdom of Ann Sokolowski

Reba Linker

AN ARTHUR KURZWEIL BOOK
New York/Jerusalem

AN ARTHUR KURZWEIL BOOK
11 Bond Street #456
Great Neck, NY 11021

First edition

Photos courtesy of Michelle Sokolowski, Elyse Fradkin, Dinah Rimler, and Reba Linker.
Illustrations and cover art by Reba Linker.

Contact Reba@RebaLinker.com.
Sign up for Reba's free newsletter at www.RebaLinker.com.
Follow Reba's blog at www.RebaLinker.com.
Like us at www.facebook.com/FollowtheYarn2013
and at www.facebook.com/pages/Reba-Linker-Author.

Reba Linker
Follow the Yarn
The Knitting Wit & Wisdom of Ann Sokolowski

ISBN: 978-0-9855658-6-2

Handmade is not homemade.
Do it right and wear it with pride!
— *Ann Sokolowski*

*A portion of the proceeds from this book will be donated to the
Celiac Disease Center at Columbia University
in honor of Ann Sokolowski.*

Table of Contents

Acknowledgements

Early on in Ann Sokolowski's beginning knitting class, a small voice within me piped up. "I want to write about Ann," it said. I kept very still, hoping the voice would go away. I ignored it for weeks, even months. The last thing I needed was another enthusiasm, another unfinished project. I had plenty of those, including the mother of all unfinished projects, an ABD (All But Dissertation) from U.C. Berkeley.

Ignoring the voice did not help. Somehow the idea had taken hold. So here I am, writing about Ann's class and writing about my unexpected adventure following the enticements of that voice in my head.

What made this project different from all the other unfinished projects in my file cabinet? I give credit to my friends who read the manuscript at various stages and gave me their invaluable ideas and insights. Most important, they gave me courage to see what needed to be done.

When in my 20s I used to sculpt, I had the pleasure of sharing studio space with other artists. It was, to me, an ideal creative situation. On breaks we would wander over to each other's workspaces. Once, a friend looked at my work, a kind of two-headed face, and said: "I think I see another face in there." Her comment gave me the courage to lop off a big chunk of rock and reveal the face that was waiting to be uncovered. Having friends is the greatest thing in the world, especially such immensely talented friends as mine who can help me see what is sometimes hidden just out of sight.

I wish to thank Janice Rimler, Sarah Cerullo, and Charles Kramer for their careful reading of the manuscript; their input helped move the project forward at crucial stages. Anoush Mardjanian, Mich-I-El Murkofsky, Chaya Ostrow, and Dinah Rimler deserve Medals of Friendship for being privy to many midnight readings of new materials. With the greatest kindness, they took my early, unpolished drafts seriously; they encouraged me to go further, and, better still, they laughed at my jokes!

Ann's daughter, Michelle Sokolowski, contributed the Foreword and gave me invaluable access to additional biographical information about Ann. I warmly thank her for her generous support of this project. Thanks to Elyse Fradkin for her wonderful photographs, to Avraham and Chana Respler for their assistance with the photo shoot, and to Judie Tulli for the beautiful layout design and cover art. In addition, Dinah Rimler and Michelle Sokolowski kindly allowed me to use their photos; their contributions greatly enhance the book.

To Ann I owe the gift of inspiration; my gratitude to her is knitted into every page. My editor, Wendy Bernstein, together with Arthur Kurzweil, the book's "midwife," enabled me to take the project to an exciting new level; with utmost kindness and enthusiasm, they made the process of "birthing" the book an adventure in discovery and achievement. Last but not least, I thank my son for his patience and love, and my husband for his loving support throughout this project, and always.

A sampling of Ann's knit projects, most made for her daughter, Michelle

Foreword

For as long as I could remember, my mother was always working on a project. Whether it was a hat, scarf, blanket, or sweater, there was always something. These projects were mostly knitting. I once asked why she didn't crochet as much and she said it was because my grandmother was so good at it. That's probably the reason I never became much of a knitter. I made some potholders and started some socks, but never had the motivation to excel. I knew I could never become as good as my mother was.

Many of these projects were made for me when I was younger and even though they no longer fit I still remember them vividly — a red sleeveless sweater with a wreath and the word Joy knitted on the front for the holidays, a light blue fuzzy sweater to match my ice-skating outfit, and a fuchsia sweater dress with a nubbly lamb on the front.

Michelle Sokolowski wearing the sleeveless sweater made for her by her mother

If we had to go somewhere that involved waiting, it was a given the knitting bag came with. And there is probably not a yarn store on the Eastern Seaboard that I was not dragged to. *Dragged* might not be the correct term. There was a little fun, mostly because we went back to the same ones and got to know the owners and other customers. But there were definitely more exciting options for an eight-year-old.

At one point my mother was the president of the Long Island Knitting Guild, which met at the Port Washington Library. I think I sat in on a meeting or two and then decided it wasn't for me — which was fine because it allowed me to bother the librarians with questions and freely roam, picking out more books than I could possibly carry home.

As I got older my mother continued to make things for me, many of which I still have today — including sweaters, hats, and scarves. These are among my favorite things in my wardrobe today.

I know how much my mother enjoyed teaching others, especially most recently her class at the Central Queens Y. I'm so happy that my mother's stories and techniques will be preserved for posterity, allowing even more people to enjoy the art of knitting.

— *Michelle Sokolowski*
August 2012

Preface

This project came into my life at a time of personal transition. Both my parents were gravely ill as I wrote. My dad passed away two years ago, and my mother one year later.

These events form the background against which Ann's gift of trust appeared as such a miracle of an opening. This book, started as a lighthearted collection of knitting notes, became, through a mysterious concatenation of events, a vehicle for the exercise of my new-found voice. A bit of my own story thus shares the pages with the lessons I learned from Ann. I did not originally plan to knit together two such divergent strands within this book; the resulting fabric has surprised even me.

The events that occurred as I was writing were the catalyst to a shift in perspective. They formed a turning point, one of those situations that not only opened a new direction, but allowed everything that went before to make sense in a new way. Though I would not have said so at the time, before that point so many things in my life had been unclear, even to me. I was busy, I was productive, and yet I had niggling doubts about my motivations, and frustrations about my outcomes. Like looking at the reverse side of fancy knit work, I could not make out the pattern or purpose. All this time I had been creating a pattern, every episode in my life supporting its creation; it gives me great joy to finally be able to turn over the fabric, to see the other side, and understand the pattern of what I had been so busily creating.

Ann played a crucial role in my personal transformation as her generosity and trust became the tool for the healing of a long-held trauma. Ann's trust issued an invitation to speak that I seem to have been waiting for all my life. As a child, I had learned not to speak about things that mattered; in a house full of embattled individuals, there did not seem to be room for one more family member to require anything. My role was to give, not take, to make others laugh, to reflect well on them. Nothing was permitted to disturb the image of the happy family, even, incredibly, through my father's three marriages and two divorces. The deceptions poisoned much that was good and added layers of confusion, self-doubt, and betrayal to my experience.

What a contrast to my connection with Ann. Sitting in her class I felt seen, recognized in a way that has been rare in my life. When I asked Ann if I could write about her and she freely granted me permission, that precious feeling of recognition blossomed into an even more substantial gift of trust and authority: I was *authorized* to be the *author* of Ann's book. I was authorized to speak, to tell my unique version of this story.

My long-suppressed voice leapt at the opening like a garrulous guest bursting into the polite society of a tea party. In my own family I felt mute, silenced. In contrast, Ann allowed me to tell her story in my words, in my way.

As a child, I had dreamed of a fairytale ending. Instead, the moral of my story is to stand up for myself, to speak up. So be it. I have so much to be thankful for. Part of the deal I made with myself was to accept what wanted to be written (even if it sometimes made me wince), to allow the project to develop in the direction that it led me. Contrasts and confluences with my personal experience resonated as I began the task of setting Ann's teachings in writing. Ann's openhanded permission allowed me to "follow the yarn" in the most unexpected directions. Winding my way through reams of knitting notes, following the thread of what so inspired me about Ann's class, to my surprise the yarn led back to me.

At times it seems like my life has been dedicated to untangling the knots of my childhood. It is a relief, finally, to unwind the myths, unravel the illusions, and arrive at a core of truth. Unwinding, unraveling to get to — what? What is at the core of a ball of yarn? There is nothing there at all. It is all just yarns, just stories. Only now, no longer muffled and bound by other people's stories, at last, my truth, too, has a voice, a strand in the fabric.

It has taken a long time, but I am finally learning how to share my authentic self with others. I am grateful to have achieved a good measure of happiness with a wonderful family of my own, and I am grateful to those in my life who accept me for who I am. Ann allowed me the opportunity to transmit her teachings and to share something of myself on these pages as well. In doing so, she provided my soul a much-needed lift just when I needed it most, and my soul joyfully leapt onboard. Ann's trust, encouragement, and acceptance have been precious gifts indeed.

— Reba Linker
February 2013

If you have knowledge,
let others light their candles at it.
— *Margaret Fuller*

1

Beginning the Yarn

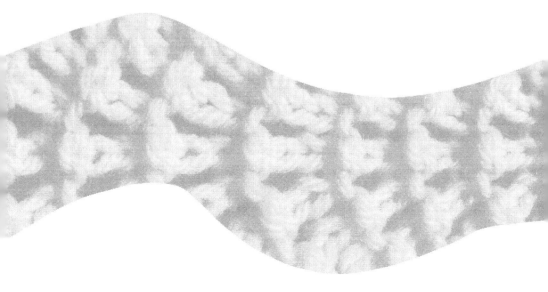

MY DEAR FRIEND Chaya always has good ideas. Together we've tried exercise classes, charitable work, and other adventures, mostly at her instigation. She is a *doer*, a woman of vast modesty and overwhelming accomplishments and any project with her is a pleasure. One day, she suggested we try a beginner knitting class starting up at our local community center, the Central Queens Y.

I went along just for the heck of it. I had no expectations and no special interest in knitting. I was keeping Chaya company, I was looking for something to do. So, on a sunny autumn day Chaya and I, along with an assorted gaggle of women and one man, assembled to check out the new knitting class.

With barely an introduction, the instructor, Ann Sokolowski, took full control of the situation, acting as if she already knew us, scolding one, and teasing another. Here, I thought, was a New York original, with the typical New Yorker's gruff exterior. She reminded me of my high school teachers: "Yo" was their preferred form of address. I later discovered that Ann had spent many years in that role and, as with my favorite teachers, I detected kindness, caring, and intelligence through the wise-guy facade.

Ann's tough bluff either chased people away (a few disappeared after the first class) or it put them wholly at ease. I was firmly in the second camp, immediately drawn to Ann's take-charge personality. This was a woman of decided opinions, expressed in no uncertain terms. A woman comfortable in her own skin, with little concern for political correctness.

I was fascinated by Ann's uncanny ability to connect with others through the most unassuming of means: a beginner's knitting class. There was something exciting happening here. The low-key, almost subversive greatness of Ann's class spoke to me of an anti-celebrity-culture, fiercely independent definition of a life well spent.

Am I reading in more than was really there? Are there gems glistening among the tangles of yarn? You decide.

> *Ann's tough bluff either chased people away or it put them wholly at ease.*

3

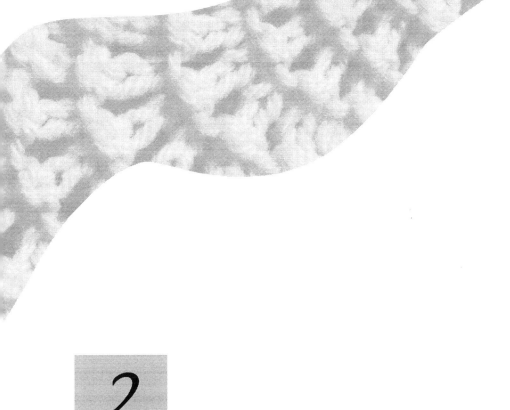

2

Washing & Drying

AT THE FIRST MEETING our group was itching to get our hands on some wool, yet there was not a scrap of yarn in sight. Instead, Ann held us back and talked about washing knitwear.

Ann was fanatic about washing knit products before gifting or wearing them. In her own life, Ann struggled with health challenges that made her sensitive to certain chemical substances. Her awareness made her especially vigilant when it came to baby gifts.

She washed to rid the yarn of any formaldehyde (!) or other sizing (the starch or chemical that gives clothes and yarn that new feel and finish) that the manufacturer may have used. She washed to get out any dirt or oils that may have accumulated from handling while knitting.

Ann had no problem giving a pre-washed gift: It was a teachable moment! At the very least, she would not hesitate to admonish the recipient to wash the gift before using and — knowing her passion for sharing information — give exact directions on how to best get the job done.

To Agitate or Not to Agitate

Correct washing gives knitted fabric suppleness and longevity. When washing wool, cashmere, and other natural fibers, move the fabric in the water as little as possible so as not to damage the fibers. Hand wash or use the gentlest machine cycle possible.

Unless a garment is stained, simply allow it to soak with minimal or no agitation. Gently squeeze out the water; do not twist or wring knitted fabric. Soak and repeat until all the soap is removed.

Use Soap, Not Detergent

Ann emphasized that clothes stay cleaner when washed in soap rather than detergent. Detergents strip fabric of its natural oils — including the lanolin in wool — making it dry and brittle. She warned against using commercial wool and fine-washable detergents. These detergents are advertised as being specifically designed for washing wool and delicates, but beware! Even hand soap is preferable to detergent when washing natural fibers such as wool and cashmere.

Ann recommended Dr. Bronner's liquid castile soap — "three squeezes per wash" — as her formula. Dr. Bronner's can be found in health food stores. It is available in many different scents, as well as unscented.

She believed that Dr. Bronner's eucalyptus-scented liquid castile soap helped rid garments of microscopic dust mites that naturally accumulate. She suggested using the eucalyptus-scented castile soap wash once per month for knitwear that is worn regularly.

I WAS INTRIGUED. You've got to love someone, I thought, who starts a knitting class with a lecture on washing knitted fabric. I relished Ann's soup-to-nuts attention to her subject. I have had my own battles with allergies and I appreciated Ann's awareness of the issue of chemical sensitivities. Further, I delighted in her colorfully emphatic style. "Etch this on your eyeballs!" she would exclaim, and follow with advice that was always backed up with a good explanation.

But most of all, I was moved. Ann's lecture made a statement that went far beyond her words. She regarded the knitted gifts she made for her extended family as heirlooms to be passed down through generations. As such, their care was as essential as their creation.

Through her attitude toward her work, and by extension toward our work as well, Ann elevated the simple notion of knitting. The work of our hands, *of my hands*, was a legacy to be cherished.

All this was accomplished through a lecture on washing knitwear. I sat up and took note: This class was going to be something special. Ann's tone may have been down to earth — salty, even — but her message was purely uplifting.

First Wash

For the first wash of any knits, but most especially baby items, Ann recommended adding one cup of borax, Borateem, baking soda, or washing soda to the wash water to remove formaldehyde and soften the yarn. (Note: I have since learned that while baking soda is fine for synthetics, it is not generally recommended for natural fibers.)

Shrinkage

According to Ann, shrinkage in the wash is caused not by temperature, but by the difference in temperature between the wash and rinse cycles. Use warm/warm or cold/cold, but do not mix two different temperatures.

Of course, do not put wool garments in a hot or warm dryer. They will shrink

Before washing

After washing

White Vinegar

Ann favored natural, pantry-shelf solutions over commercial chemical products. She took a tip from the traditional dyer's art: Prevent dark and bright-colored yarns from bleeding their color in the wash or on the wearer's body. For the first wash, use 1 cup of white vinegar in rinse water to set the color.

White vinegar is also a natural fabric softener. Use it instead of chemical softeners, which may damage natural fibers.

Over-Dyed Yarns

Ann collected arcane tidbits about her craft. This one gave her another log to throw on the wash-it-before-you-use-or-gift-it! fire. She explained that when a batch of, say, pink, goes awry, rather than try to correct it, the manufacturer may simply dye over the batch with a stronger color, such as red or black. The double dose of dye makes these intensely colored yarns stiff. Washing fabrics made from over-dyed colors is crucial in order to restore the yarn to its true feel.

Ironing

Never touch a hot iron directly to your work. Instead, place a cloth or tea towel over the item you are blocking or pressing. Set the iron's temperature to low, and use the steam setting. Allow the steam, rather than direct pressure or heat, to do the job.

Drying

Drying a knit garment on a hanger is a spectacularly bad idea. Draping it over a bar is bad enough (the weight of the wet wool will stretch it out) but hanging — don't go there!

Even hanging a dry sweater on a hanger is a bad idea — pointy little bumps

"This is my shape — really!"

may develop where the hanger meets the shoulders — and a wet sweater that much more so. Instead, gently squeeze out excess water and lay knitwear flat to dry, or dry 10 minutes in a cool dryer, then lay flat to dry.

All who crossed her path were treated to the same mixture of interest and concern, usually followed by some definitive advice.

WHEN I FIRST APPROACHED Ann with the idea of creating this book, she responded: "Put it in writing? I'd get arrested!"

Ann's sense of humor was a well-honed tool in her teaching arsenal. It was a strategy developed years ago when she was a novice New York City public school speech teacher facing a room full of sullen teenagers: "If they laughed," she explained, "it relieved the tension and they were not scared."

Her humor was backed by an encyclopedic knowledge of her craft. Yet the most irresistible weapon at Ann's command was her genuine engagement with others. Teens or seniors alike were intensely interesting specimens feeding a deep curiosity about the human condition. All who crossed her path were treated to the same mixture of interest and concern, usually followed by some definitive advice.

Ann (back row, center) with some of her students at John Adams High School in Queens, NY. If you look closely, you can see that they are all holding knitting in their hands.

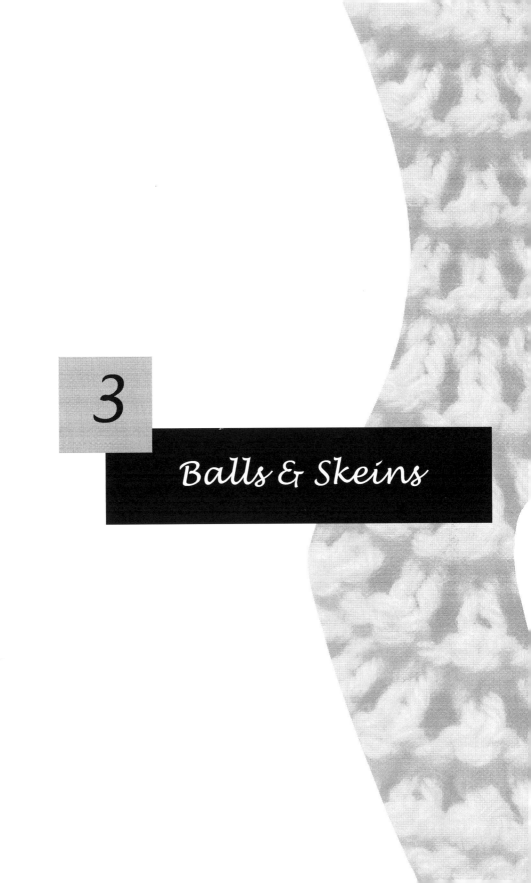

3

Balls & Skeins

ONE HALLMARK of a generous teacher is the ability to step into a beginner's shoes. Ann had that ability in spades. There were no secret handshakes — if there were, Ann would make sure we were in on them! She relished her role of guru initiating us into the mysteries of our craft. She enjoyed revealing and explaining, and she bestowed a fully rounded world of information on her students, with affection for every detail.

No topic was too elementary or too small. Ann did not assume that a student knew how to pull yarn from a skein. Indeed, how would a newcomer know that the yarn pulls best from the inside of the skein?

Unwinding the Skein of Yarn

There are two ends in every skein: One pulls from the center, the other is wrapped around the outside. The yarn feed should come from the inside of the skein — just reach in, grab some yarn from the middle, and pull it out. The yarn end will be in there!

For every tip she offered, Ann gave us the reason behind it: Pull the yarn from the inside and the skein stays put. Pull it from the outside and the skein will bounce all over as it unwinds (bouncing skein equals uneven yarn feed tension, dirty skein, hard to handle).

Zip It Up

Ann kept her ball of yarn in a Ziploc (quart- or gallon-size) bag while she knit. A two-inch opening allowed the yarn feed to come through; the rest of the bag was kept zipped up. The yarn stayed cleaner than if it was loose, rolling on the floor or picking up lint in a knitting bag. (This only works with the yarn pulled from the center, as above, or the skein will flop around like a live fish in a sack.)

Making a Ball of Yarn

Ann showed us several ways to make a ball of yarn. All are constructed so that you can pull the yarn from the inside, just as you would a store-bought skein.

To make a round ball, wrap yarn around four fingers (held like a paw, thumb not included). Leave a length of yarn (one or two feet) hanging out as you wrap. This yarn will pull from the inside and will become your yarn feed. When the yarn around your fingers starts to have some bulk to it, wrap in a new direction; never cover the pull spot, always leave the tail accessible — it will become the yarn feed. Keep wrapping in different directions to make your ball of yarn round. Tuck the last wrap into itself and now you are wrapping yarn like a pro.

For mini balls of yarn, Ann showed us how to do a quick wrap, followed by a wrap around the middle that bundles it at the "waist." It will look a little like a butterfly. Tuck the outside end into the last loop and pull it snug to secure.

For Ann knitting was a way to connect.

Ann's favorite method was a figure 8, wound around your thumb and pointer finger. Always leave the inside tail dangling out to use as the yarn feed. Finish it off by wrapping around the middle, butterfly-style, as above.

I recently heard a tip from a knitting friend, who reappeared in my life just as I was beginning to write this book, also full-throttle into fabric arts. Anoush, who happens to be a talented spinner, wraps the yarn around the handle of a wooden spoon, leaving the feed hanging as she wraps. She turns the spoon as she wraps, yet even without that skillful touch, the sweet thing is that when the spoon is removed the hollow space where the handle had been allows the yarn space to pull from the inside with ease. (This tip was too good not to share. Unless I mention otherwise, all other tips are from Ann.)

MAKING AN AFGHAN for a new baby in her extended family or sharing her knowledge with her students at the Y, for Ann knitting was a way to connect with people. Even her public school students — boys included — were initiated into the art of knitting. So contagious was her enthusiasm that her students won an award for their donation of an astonishing 700 knit caps to the needy.

Ann with some of the many bags of hats her students made for the Caps for Kids charity

The pride Ann's students must have felt in their accomplishment was as important as the knitting itself. While the knitting was purely an extra-curricular activity, Ann maintained that teaching her students to knit significantly improved their self-confidence — and their grades.

Today, knitting is used in hospitals as a therapeutic activity for both patients and their families. Yarn Alive, an Ohio-based charity, sends yarn to Japan to help tsunami victims, and a Maryland penitentiary notes a decrease in violence among inmates who participate in the Knitting Behind Bars program.

Healing, calming, empowering, focusing, creating, connecting — it seems there is more to knitting than meets the eye. Ann was way ahead of the curve on that one.

More hats made by Ann's students.
Note the clotheslines hung with hats, ready to be packed into bags.

4

Ann's Beginners Knit Sampler

OUR FIRST ASSIGNMENT was a knit sampler that we worked on over the course of several weeks. Ann was very, very clear that we would not be making a scarf or other beginner project. The sampler exemplified Ann's teaching philosophy: Experiment, explore new territory, and gain some mastery. Then, and only then, tools well in hand, embark on a project.

The sampler is your research. Tennis champion Billie Jean King puts it this way: "For me, losing a tennis match isn't failure, it's research." It is meant to be a portrait of your history, warts and all. While in the future Ann would admonish us to "Do it right and wear it with pride," for the sampler she purposefully set that notion aside.

Do not rip out and redo stitches; just keep knitting and you will gain the satisfaction of seeing your improvement when you look back on your work. The product is knowledge — to my mind, a far more useful product than a beginner hat nobody wants to wear!

My Beginners Knit Sampler — a picture of the beginning of my knitting journey, warts and all!

Samplers Are Not Just for Beginners

Ann maintained that a big chunk of your learning curve should happen outside a project, not in it. Whenever a project introduces a new variable — new stitch, unfamiliar yarn, different-sized needles — make a sampler!

Four inches is an ideal swatch size, unless, of course, your stitch needs a larger sample (i.e., if the repeat is wider than four inches). Work out the kinks in a small space before you start your project. When something is off in your project, you will recognize it easily and early.

Most commercial patterns give instructions for a sample square using the recommended yarn and needles. A pattern will indicate that a four-inch square should be so many stitches wide and so many rows high. If the knitter's square comes out per specifications, then the chances are much improved that the finished product will be true to size.

Sampler Stitches

Ann had us dedicate a few inches of our sampler — about two to four inches per stitch — to each of the following stitches:

1. Garter
2. Stockinette
3. Rib
4. Spiral Rib
5. Moss or Seed

The instructions for these stitches may be found below. When you finish your Beginners Knit Sampler, you will be ready to start your first knitted project.

ANN FORESTALLED disaster by choosing the yarn and needles for our Beginners Knit Sampler. She selected a basic worsted-weight acrylic yarn and size seven needles. She deliberately chose light colors so we could easily see what we were doing.

Ann even purchased the yarn and needles for us, which was a good way for her to stay in control and make sure we did not stray too far afield at the start. She charged us a ridiculously low fee for the supplies — $2, I think it was. It was clear Ann was not in this for the money!

Chaya had tried a knitting class in which beginner students were handed a bunch of novelty yarns — fun fur and the like — on which to learn to knit. Ann would have had a fit. She understood that the yarn selected could mean the difference between success and failure, and between a new knitting enthusiast and someone who walks away in frustration.

ANN RECEIVED A FOUNDATION of skill and pride in her craftsmanship from her seamstress mother. To this foundation, she added her own discoveries. She revised her knitting technique as an adult, explaining that she had learned it "wrong" as a child. This revelation fueled her fascination with the subject, and she continually sought out the best people in the field for their expertise.

Ann's love of craft was coupled with a gift for communication. She was hooked in high school, when a favorite teacher convinced her to stand up and speak in front of people, and Ann "began to realize the fun in public speaking and in trying to influence an audience."

(Note her choice of the word "influence" — Ann was a born pedagogue!) This discovery set the direction for her career as a speech teacher.

As a high school senior, Ann won a writing contest sponsored by *The News*. The essay, "2 Weeks in the Country," is vintage Ann, poking fun at the absurdity of human behavior, and at the same time including herself in the joke as one of those humans who couldn't resist two weeks in the country among the flies, bees, mosquitoes, broken lawn chairs, and busted water pipes. A philosopher with a populist touch, Ann wrote as if looking down from above, tickled by human contradictions, and yet at the same time one with the subjects of her study, fully sharing in their foibles. She was then, as ever, a blue-collar Yoda.

In an interview from her days as a high school speech teacher, it is easy to recognize the same Ann we met at the Y: enjoying the way her students could surprise her, coaching the drama club, opining on music and culture, and mobilizing to improve the theater facilities. On the importance of speech as a subject, she did not mince words: "If you can't communicate with your fellow man, you are nothing."

Throughout much of her career, Ann stayed close to her roots and family. She graduated from St. Joseph's College for Women in 1963 with a major in speech and a minor in English. In 1965 she returned to teach speech at her high school alma mater, John Adams High School in Queens, NY, where her uncle also attended and her sister taught history.

After a break from teaching in 1967, Ann returned to John Adams High School in 1968. The next year she became assistant dean, and then dean. (By the way, Ann never mentioned these accomplishments; I only found out by chance when looking through some papers while preparing this book. This reticence was not due to any great sense of modesty; rather, it reflected a rare ethical rigor: Each individual, including herself, was to be taken on the merits of his or her actions — words and deeds — not on past actions or titles. Besides, no title could possibly confer any greater authority than that which Ann already granted herself. She was supremely confident and authoritative in all her interactions.)

Ann taught at John Adams until her retirement in the mid-1990s. In 1996 she returned to her college alma mater, St Joseph's, as an adjunct faculty member to teach oral communication.

> *"If you can't communicate with your fellow man, you are nothing."*

5

Yarn Feed & Knit Gauge

IT MAY SEEM odd to start learning to knit before learning how to cast on (that is, before learning how to get the loops on the knitting needle in the first place), yet this was how Ann taught us. For those who did not know how to cast on, Ann would cast on for them. Her idea was to start knitting, to catch the rhythm of the thing before getting tangled up in the mechanics of casting on.

Ann taught the Continental style of knitting, in which the yarn feed is held in the left hand. The Continental style enables an efficient action and an ease of switching from knit to purl, as opposed to the American style, in which the right hand carries the yarn feed over the needle.

It was Ann's belief that the Continental style produced a more even product. One of her students, Dinah, had been using the American style all her life. Although it was hard to change, when she finally did, Dinah felt that, sure enough, the Continental style produced a superior product. This was high praise indeed from a woman who was already an expert knitter for many years before she met Ann.

If a student was committed to the American style, Ann did not pressure her to change. Most of her advice applied to whatever style of knitting a student preferred.

Your Hold as You Knit

Knitting uses fine-muscle articulation rather than gross movement. If your hands get tired, cramped, or stiff from knitting, your grip is too tight. Ann liked to massage her hands to keep them soft, flexible, and relaxed.

If your elbow is moving up and down while you knit, you are using the wrong muscles. Hold your arms still; let the smaller muscles in the hand do the work.

Her idea was to start knitting, to catch the rhythm of the thing before getting tangled up in the mechanics of casting on.

ANN TOLD US THE STORY of the time her arm was in a cast and she took up a knitting project during her recuperation. It was a small project, using lightweight yarn, so as not to overtax her injured arm.

When the cast was removed the doctors were astonished at

her recovery. Ann claims that it was due to the fine-muscle workout entailed in knitting. If Ann had held the needle in what she called a "death grip," the exercise would not have been possible, let alone therapeutic.

If you are breaking a sweat, you may need to rethink your technique.

The Feel of Proper Gauge
Knitted fabric should have a spring and stretch to it. It should feel bouncy. If your knitting comes out flimsy, floppy, and stretched out, you are holding your needles and yarn feed too loosely. If your knitting comes out stiff and tight, the opposite is true.

Gauge literally means the number of stitches per row (vertically and horizontally) needed to achieve the optimal fabric texture. Gauge is affected by a combination of factors: the thickness and texture of the wool, the size of the needles, the type of stitch, and the tension of the knitter's grip.

Gauge is important not just for the feel of the thing. It is crucial to the fit of a garment when following a pattern — hence the need to make a sample square to test for gauge before beginning a project.

Holding the Yarn Feed
Start by winding the yarn around your left pinkie once and then your left forefinger. The yarn feed will be held behind the left needle for knit stitches, and in front of the left needle for purl stitches.

The yarn around the left pinkie helps control the tension of the yarn feed. The yarn should be able to flow out as you knit without having to stop and re-adjust.

There are many variations. Some people prefer to wrap the feed twice around the forefinger. See what feels right for you. The hold may also need adjusting according to the slipperiness of the yarn, the dryness or moisture of your hand, the weather, etc.

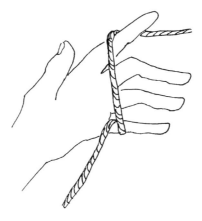

Ann's preferred yarn feed hold: around the pinkie and then the forefinger.

6

Tell Me a Stitch:
Knit & Purl

ANN WOULD HARDLY ever show us how to do a stitch. Rather, she would insist that we repeat her instructions out loud, step by step, and try to "do it as we spoke it." She wanted us to find our way by hearing, thinking, and doing rather than by seeing. She wanted us to discover a technique for ourselves rather than copy it.

This teaching technique was oddly frustrating. It was also fascinating how at times it seemed to take a lot of courage just to try something new — even something as incidental as a new stitch. (Through the loop? Like this? Dare I? Really?)

In the end, I think Ann's method gave us confidence in a way that spoon-feeding us answers might not have done. Learning a new stitch, our class would buzz with curiosity, excitement, nervousness, and accomplishment.

If we were really frustrated, Ann suggested consulting online tutorials. She had no hesitation using the Internet's wealth of knitting websites.

ANN LIKED TO SAY: "There are only two stitches in knitting: the knit and purl," abbreviated as K and P, respectively. All, yes *all*, of the variations are based on those two stitches. Master the knit and purl stitches and you have mastered the fundamental tools of the craft.

Full disclosure: There may not even be two stitches in knitting. As you get to know them, you may begin to see the knit and purl as the front and back of the same stitch.

Knit Stitch

Ann gave us four steps in four sentences:

1. In the loop, front to back
2. Down on the yarn
3. Pull it through the loop
4. Off the needle

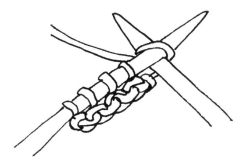

The right needle enters the loop on the left side of the loop, going front to back.

We struggled mightily to make sense of it. Here again are the same four sentences, with a bit more explanation:

Ann's presence — that gift to us of her time and energy — was the subtext of every lesson.

---

1. In the loop, front to back:
With the yarn feed held behind the left needle, the right needle enters to the left of the loop. It goes from left to right, front to back, under the left needle, through the loop.

2. Down on the yarn:
Going over the top and behind the yarn feed, hook the yarn as if making a comma with your needle point.

3. Pull it through the loop:
There should be a new loop on the right needle, pulled through the old loop on the left needle.

4. Off the needle:
The right needle pulls the old loop off the left needle; after that there should be one additional loop on the right needle and one fewer loop on the left needle.

WHEN I FINALLY got to see Ann knitting (weeks after she taught us the knit and purl stitches), a glimpse of her in action answered a multitude of questions. I was amazed at the elasticity of her movement. She really stretched the loops as she knitted.

This encouraged me to experiment with my stitches as well. The loops can really take some pulling. Because knitting is such a mass of interlocking movable parts, everything seems to spring back into shape and even out in the end.

SEEING ANN KNIT confirmed for me the notion that nothing should fully replace hands-on passing of technique. Aside from the practical advantages of being able to ask questions, see a thing from various angles, go at your own pace, etc., the unique unrecorded, unduplicated experience of one-on-one, live human interaction could well be a new definition of luxury in today's world.

Ann's presence — that gift to us of her time and energy —

was the subtext of every lesson. This book invites you to share in all that we received from Ann, and pick and choose from among her copious tips. Yet, do not let this book be your only knitting companion. If at all possible, find the real-time, real-live human connection, and let the art and craft of knitting be passed — in the time-honored fashion — face to face and hand to hand.

The idea that I am part of a chain of skill that has been handed down for generations excites my imagination, and I am grateful to all in that lineage. Like Ann, I learned to knit "wrong" as a child. Though I had long forgotten the stitch, the message of capability conveyed to me by my mother's hands remained. Having learned to knit as a child made knitting feel familiar when I relearned it the "right way" with Ann.

Purl

Again, Ann gave us four steps in four sentences:
1. Needle in, back to front (on inside)
2. Down on the yarn — stabilizing with thumb on the yarn
3. Pull through the loop
4. Off the needle

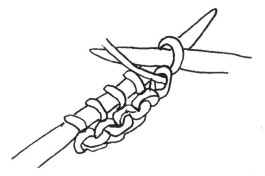

The right needle stays in front, going from the right side of the loop to the left.

Here are Ann's instructions with a bit more elaboration:
1. Needle in, back to front (on inside):
With the yarn feed held in front of the left needle, the right needle enters the front part of the loop from right to left.

2. Down on the yarn — stabilizing with thumb on the yarn:
Like an upside down comma, the right needle moves from under the yarn feed, up and around in front of it to grab it.

3. Pull through the loop:
There should be a new loop on the right needle, pulled through the old loop on the left needle.

33

4. Off the needle:
The right needle pulls the old loop off the left needle; after that there should be one additional loop on the right needle and one fewer loop on the left needle.

Ann maintained that one did not need to use the left finger to assist with catching the yarn feed and pulling it through when doing a purl stitch. However, I use my left pointer finger to help, and cannot see how to do it otherwise.

UNLIKE MANY KNITTING GROUPS, which tend to function in the egalitarian style of a quilting bee, Ann kept a firm grip on the reins of her class, scowling at interruptions and demanding our full attention. Many days she would hardly let us knit; she would just pour out her knowledge as we scribbled notes and scrambled to keep up.

The information was not always sequential, nor even topical. Some days we hardly even talked about knitting. Among my notes I stumble upon Ann's recipe for flourless peanut butter cookies, as well as the homeopathic remedies she swore by.

If you answered anything other than "fine" to Ann's "How ya doin'?" she might well go into a long digression on whatever ailed you (or your friend, or your relative), and regale you with similar episodes from her extensive repertoire of anecdotes. (Not all the stories were flattering: Several involved homeopathic cures for hangovers!)

If Ann found it to be good, she shared it. It all tumbled out in an avalanche of information she had accrued over a lifetime not just of knitting, but of *living*.

At times it felt like we were standing still, yet despite the digressions, I find when I review my notes that there was an incredible amount of information. It just came out Ann's way. The remedies, the recipes, the anecdotes, the knitting information — all were part of her accumulated knowledge, and we were the chosen recipients.

Some individuals may have been frustrated with Ann's style, and they gradually moved away from the class. But a small core group recognized her genius, and we chose her in return.

7

Beginners Knit Sampler Stitches

O<small>UR</small> BEGINNERS KNIT sampler used basic stitch patterns, all variations in the order and combination of knit and purl stitches. Ann wanted us to have a sense of each stitch's utility, and I have tried to include that here as well.

If knitting instructions sound complicated, there is good reason: Simple as a thing may be, there are many ways to get it wrong. (On the flip side, those many ways of getting it wrong are the keys to lovely variations, but more on that later.) Often, the simplest action takes 10 times longer to read about than to do.

As with any foreign language, fluency takes practice. Do not feel obliged to absorb all the information presented. It is part of what Ann gave us, here if you want it. (For those interested, additional stitches and variations that Ann gave us that were not included in the Beginners Knit Sampler may be found in Appendix B.)

Garter Stitch
Knit every row. Ta-da! You are knitting!

Garter stitch lies flat (i.e., it des not curl), so it makes a useful border to a scarf or afghan. It produces rows of purl-y bumps with a subtle horizontal stripe and is somewhat bulky.

The words *bulky* and *horizontal stripes* may flash warning signals for some fashionistas. On the other hand, that heft is the very reason Ann chose the garter stitch for a baby blanket she was working on. She wanted the blanket to be used as a play area on the floor; garter stitch provided the right amount of cushioning for the baby.

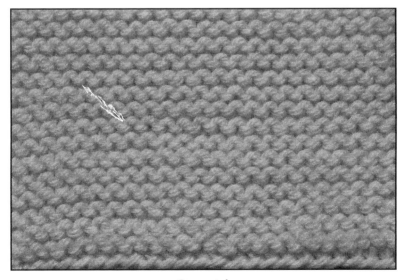

Garter stitch

GARTER STITCH PATTERN:

All rows: Knit to end of row

Repeat to desired length

The Garter Stitch Proof-of-the-One-Stitch Hypothesis

Supporting the notion that there is only one stitch in knitting, and knit and purl are two sides of the same stitch, garter stitch can be achieved by purling rather than knitting both sides. Purled garter stitch should look exactly the same as knitted garter stitch.

Stockinette Stitch

Stockinette alternates knit and purl rows, producing a smooth fabric with the classic, supple knit look.

With stockinette comes the concept of a *right* side and *wrong* side — a front and back of a knit fabric, abbreviated as RS and WS, respectively. The right side is the knit side, with vertical rows of stitches that look like the letter V. The wrong side is the purl side, with horizontal rows of purl-y bumps. Of course, there are exceptions to every rule: When a pattern calls for the purl-y side to be the right side, it is referred to as *reverse stockinette*.

Stockinette curls at the edges. In a seamed garment this is not an issue. For flat items, such as an afghan or scarf, tame the curl by adding a noncurling border, such as garter.

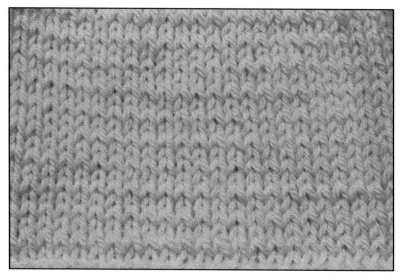

Stockinette stitch, knit side (right side)

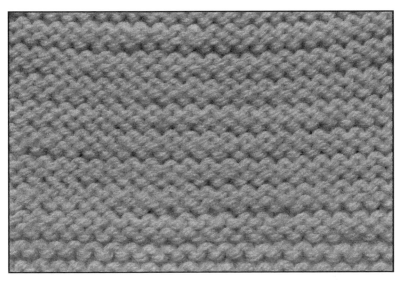

Stockinette stitch, purl side (wrong side, or reverse stockinette)

The Stockinette Test of Stitch Consistency

I hate to call attention to a flaw; nonetheless, I altruistically mention it to share Ann's useful indicator of stitch consistency. Ann pointed out that the dark horizontal lines in the wrong side stockinette sample, above, ideally shouldn't be there. They indicate unevenness in the tension of the stitches. A good reverse stockinette should look as smooth as machine-made. I haven't mastered it, but I have seen it and it is really impressive.

> STOCKINETTE STITCH PATTERN:
> Row 1 and all odd-numbered rows (RS): Knit to end of row
> Row 2 and all even rows (WS): Purl to end of row
> Repeat to desired length

Rib Stitch

Rib stitch alternates columns of knit Vs with columns of purl-y bumps. The columns — or ribs — can be as narrow as one stitch, or as wide as five stitches or more. The happy result of these alternating columns is that the knit columns pull forward and the purl columns recede. This creates an accordion-like bunching in the fabric, which gives it great stretchiness.

Rib stitch is useful for cuffs, collars, and sweater bottoms. It can also be used for entire garments. Ribbed sweaters are naturally form-fitting; Ann's hat project (see page 133) is an all-rib cap. Ribbing can even be used to give cotton — which has less spring-back than wool — some elasticity.

Rib stitch with two-stitch wide columns

RIB STITCH PATTERN:
(Two-stitch-wide columns)
Cast on in multiples of four stitches
All rows: K2, P2 to end of row
Repeat to desired length

Spiral Rib Stitch
Like the rib stitch, the spiral rib stitch makes a stretchy, ribbed fabric, with the added element that every four rows the columns move over a notch. As the columns jog to the left, it creates the illusion of a diagonal spiral. Fun!

With spiral rib, Ann showed us how we could step up the complexity and visual interest of a stitch we already knew by making a small tweak in the pattern. While the stitches remain basic knit and purl, the pattern suddenly becomes a bit of a mind-bender.

Spiral rib stitch

SPIRAL RIB STITCH PATTERN:

Cast on in multiples of four stitches

Rows 1-4: (K2, P2) to end of row

Row 5: P1, *(K2, P2) repeat from * to end of row; end K1

Row 6: K1, *(P2, K2) repeat from * to end of row; end P1

Row 7: Same as Row 5

Row 8: Same as Row 6

Rows 9-12: (P2, K2) to end of row

Row 13: K1, *(P2, K2) repeat from * to end of row; end P1

Row 14: P1, *(K2, P2) repeat from * to end of row; end K1

Row 15: Same as Row 13

Row 16: Same as Row 14

Repeat rows 1-16 to the desired length

* = repeat starts from the asterisk

Moss (aka Seed) Stitch

The moss stitch creates an even texture of pronounced bumps. It is reversible and, because it lies flat, it is useful for edges. Moss stitch simply alternates stitches, one purl, one knit.

41

Moss stitch

MOSS STITCH PATTERN:
Cast on in multiples of two stitches
Row 1: (K1, P1) repeat to end of row
Row 2: (P1, K1) repeat to end of row
Repeat rows 1 and 2 to desired length

What Presents
The sampler stitches enabled Ann to introduce the concept of *what presents*. Grasp this concept and your ability skyrockets.

By using visual cues, specifically, distinguishing between knit Vs and purl-y bumps (rather than counting stitches), you can easily stay on pattern. Per your pattern, either do what presents, or do the opposite of what presents — that is, knit where you see a knit V and purl where you see a purl-y bump, or purl where you see a knit V and knit where you see a purl-y bump.

Rib and moss stitch both alternate knit and purl stitches, yet they part company when it comes to doing what presents. To make the columns characteristic of rib stitch, do what presents. To create the bumps characteristic of moss stitch, do the opposite of what presents.

Double Moss Stitch
Double moss alternates two purl stitches and two knit stitches. Like moss, it is fully reversible.

Double moss stitch

DOUBLE MOSS PATTERN:

Cast on in multiples of four stitches
Row 1: (K2, P2) repeat to end of row
Row 2: (P2, K2) repeat to end of row
Repeat rows 1 and 2 to desired length

WHEN WE MET in October 2009, it was evident that Ann was not in the best of health. She used a walker, and had mentioned celiac disease, missing toes, and an exposure to Agent Orange, though we never got the full details. The driver who brought Ann to class every week was not a luxury, but a necessity. The few times the elevator at the Y was out of service meant either finding a room on the ground floor or canceling the class. Stairs were out of the question.

I suspect that Ann's health affected the way she ran her class. Her vision was not always reliable — which may be one reason we were rarely treated to watching her knit. I later found out that Ann's visual difficulty was due to diabetic retinopathy. Of course, she turned this frailty into an asset, making a pedagogical point of having us use our ears and brains rather than our eyes!

Her health issues may also explain her organization of the class, and her distractedness. Some days must have been harder than others. Yet she was there, on time, always eager to share her knowledge with the group.

43

WHY DID ANN TEACH at the Y? It was a volunteer position. She commuted at considerable expense and trouble to herself, hiring a car and driver, and she was there without financial remuneration.

Certainly, Ann had something of value she wanted to share. Perhaps, too, she needed us as much as we needed her. Unlike many people, Ann relieved her loneliness by giving rather than by taking.

Ann had something of value she wanted to share. Perhaps, too, she needed us as much as we needed her.

8

Side, Bottom &
Top & Edges

EXPERIENCED KNITTERS like Dinah, Tina, Christena, and others came to

Ann for the tips she offered in such abundance. To a knitter, those tips were pure gold.

Side Edges

Ann's "etch this on your eyelids" rule: ALWAYS add two stitches when casting on. Every row, slip the first stitch and knit the last stitch for smooth side edges.

Ann swore by this technique. A good edge not only looks neat, it also helps you to sew a flat seam. Bid adieu to the bulky seams you sometimes see in hand-knit sweaters (so irritating, especially in the armpit area! And who wants extra bulk in their silhouette, anyway?).

A regular knit edge

An edge made using Ann's rule: Slip the first stitch and knit the last stitch.

Slip as if to purl, that is, with your yarn feed in front. Your edge will look like a row of Vs, similar in appearance to the cast-on edge. If you get a row of horizontal bumps on your edge it is because you slipped as if to knit, that is, did the slip stitch with the yarn feed in back.

Keep the last knit stitch loose or the fabric will curl. It is doing double duty — working for two rows because the first stitch is just a slip stitch, that is, carried up from the previous row without an added loop.

Cast On with Large Needles

Ann commanded: "Tattoo this on your eyelids: For casting on and off, use a knitting needle two sizes larger than the one you are knitting with!" So, if your project uses a size 7 needle, use a size 9 needle to cast on, etc. Even then, do not tug the loops tight, or it will defeat the purpose.

The looser gauge of the cast on loops allows for the stretchiness needed at the edges of a garment. Cast on too tight, and the garment will weaken or rip every time the wearer pulls it on — disaster!

Some knitters prefer to cast on using two needles held together. At the opposite end of the spectrum, an experienced knitter might be able to adjust gauge by feel without using bigger needles at all.

Ann mentioned several ways to cast on. Do not get into a kerfuffle over the explanations: Get a friend to show you how! Do remember Ann's point that there are many ways to do a thing, and that different ways apply best in specific circumstances. These are not required distinctions, and most knitters can use a single method of casting on for their entire lives. Ann just wanted us to know that this level of refinement exists, if we cared to explore it.

Simple Cast On
Make a slip stitch and place it on one knitting needle.

Knit a stitch.

Instead of putting the newly created loop onto the right needle, put it on the left needle.

Repeat for as many loops you need to cast on. Just try it. It really is that simple.

Ribbed Cast On
For a K2, P2 Rib pattern:

Do the Simple Cast On (above) for two stitches.

On the third and fourth stitches: Insert the needle in between the previous two loops and continue as above (i.e., knit the stitch and place it on the left needle instead of the right needle). This comes out like a purl stitch.

Keep alternating between two Simple Cast On stitches (step 1, above) and two Purl Cast On stitches (step 2, above).

Note: Inserting the needle in between the stitches means just that — just stick the needle into the space between one stitch and another. The right needle grabs the yarn feed exactly as it would in a regular knit stitch.

Adjust the pattern as needed for wider and narrower ribs.

Long-Tailed Cast On
To learn this technique, visit the tutorial at www.knittinghelp.com/video/play/long-tail-cast-on.

This technique produces a stable cast on, more like a knit row than a series of loops. In fact, if the pattern calls for, say, two knit rows after you cast on, Ann would count the long-tailed cast on as the first knit row.

As you cast on, you must hold the tail end in front, around your thumb, or you will lose stitches.

Each cast-on loop uses about 1.5 inches of yarn, As you can imagine, it is quite difficult to premeasure or estimate the length of the tail for very large projects; running out of yarn 10 stitches short of a 300-stitch cast on is no one's idea of fun. To solve this dilemma, Ann used two balls of yarn to do the long-tailed casting on.

Start with a slipknot that holds both yarns. Use one skein as the skein you will be knitting with and the other as the tail. When you are finished casting on, snip the tail yarn (of course leaving a 6-8-inch tail to bury later), and start knitting.

Casting Off
Casting off (aka binding off or dropping off) is the most common way to end a piece and get the last row of loops off your knitting needles.

K1, P1, or Slip 1 to start (choose one, as per your pattern) and then stick with that and don't vary.

K1, P1, or Slip 1 again.

Pass the old stitch (on your right needle) over the new one (also on the right needle) and drop it off.

Continue repeating steps 2 and 3. There should always be one or two stitches only on the right needle.

When a single loop remains on the right needle, pull the tail through the loop, leaving a 6-inch tail to bury.

WHETHER OR NOT we managed to accomplish the day's lesson plan (if there was one), I loved being there.

Ann seemed to take the measure of each person with a piercingly accurate mental yardstick. Some folks she teased ("You! Go sit in the corner!" was a repeated refrain to one of her most devoted students), others were handled more gently, and still others were practically chased away.

She saved her particular wrath for an instructor who marched through our classroom on her way to her supply closet; apparently, the instructor did not exhibit enough awareness of Ann's claim on the space, and Ann, ever the lioness, growled at her every time she passed through.

She rarely teased me or even interacted much with me in class. Yet in a way that has been rare in my experience, I felt recognized — truly seen — in her presence.

What does that mean, *seen*? My friend Anoush asked, "OK, the class was sometimes disorganized, she wasn't always pleasant, so what were we doing there?"

I was there — I've come to understand now — because I felt recognized, quietly understood. And when I say that, I specifically mean recognized for good, recognized as good. Validated.

In the Jewish tradition, there is an admonition to *heker hatov* — "to see the good" — as a daily practice, to consciously and conscientiously seek out the positive in every situation, rather than focusing on the negative. In retrospect, I had been going through a dark period in which I felt little trust, little sharing, little faith coming from the people around me, no matter how I tried to merit their trust and care. As a result, I doubted myself; I felt untrustworthy, undeserving, disregarded, dishonored. At that moment, Ann's simple gaze of respect was a hand held out in the darkness to pull me toward the light.

Ann *heker*ed *hatov* in me, easily, naturally. Though I didn't realize it at the time, that is what drew me to write about her, and that is the key to what became such a source of healing for me. Ann saw the good in me, and that enabled me to see the good in myself and, ultimately, even to see the good in all that

> *As I sat in class, I felt Ann's recognition as a thread connecting us, a steady hum that sang beneath the clatter of teasing and technique.*

51

had happened to me — even the hardships, perhaps even especially the hardships.

Ann and I never spoke about personal matters. We didn't call each other up to chat (though she gave out her phone number and invited us all to use it). Yet as I sat in class, I felt Ann's recognition as a thread connecting us, a steady hum that sang beneath the clatter of teasing and technique. I felt surrounded by an aura of acceptance, confidence, and trust. I get a lump in my throat when I think about it. And I have to chuckle. Here I am, welling up at some bossy lady telling me to etch some knitting technique on my eyelids!

The universe works in mysterious ways. Go figure.

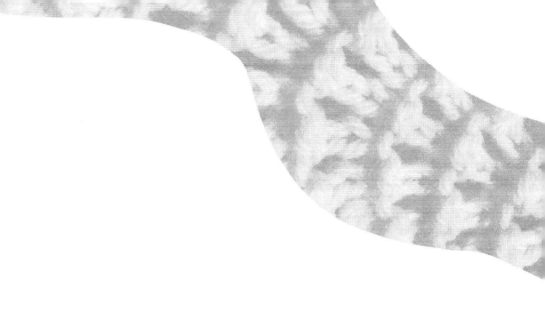

9

Increases
& Decreases

ONCE I HAD DECIDED to write about Ann's class, my notes were far more extensive than they might otherwise have been. The sheer quantity of information is astonishing. I count this as a life lesson in itself: How much information is available if only one takes note of it!

OUR CLASS HAD EXPLORED simple variations of knit and purl in order to create stitch patterns. Next, Ann took us to the next level: manipulating the shape of the stitches themselves, creating increases and decreases that give us tools to shape garments and create lacey effects.

Ann wanted us to know our options, she wanted us in on the game. We may not have been able to do much at first, but we could bandy about terms like *left-leaning decreases* and *pass the slip stitch over* with the best of them.

Increases — Make One

Increases add stitches as you are knitting. Make One (M1) gives an increase with a solid look to it, and is commonly used in all types of garments. Knit the front of the loop without pulling it off the needle, then knit the back of the loop, then remove both newly created (two knit stitches) loops from the needle.

To Make One in purl, simply purl the back and the front of your loop and then remove both newly created loops from the needle.

Increases — Yarn Over and Yarn Under

Yarn Over (YO) creates a hole in the garment, giving a lacy look. YO in American patterns is the same as YRN (Yarn Round Needle) in British patterns.

The gesture for YO is the same gesture used to pick up yarn in a normal knitted stitch, but without actually going through the loop. It won't look like much at first, but when you knit the next row, the YO becomes integrated into the fabric.

Ann wanted us to know our options, she wanted us in on the game.

In patterns with YOs, most often there is a purled row on the wrong side in order to stabilize the stitches.

YO may be done purl-wise as well, using the same yarn wrap direction used on a purl stitch. There are many variations to play with, such as Yarn Under (the opposite wrap direction as YO) for either purl or knit stitches, which yield slightly different shapes and widths of holes.

Increases — Knit in the Row Below
Another increase is to knit in the row below the current row, in addition to knitting the stitch in the current row. To increase in the row below purl-wise, do the same, except, of course, purl in the row below.

Decreases
Use different techniques according to the needs of your project. One of Ann's mini-samplers would be an ideal way to experiment with different types of increases and decreases.

Decreases slant left or right. Ann considered Knit Two Together (K2TOG) a right-facing decrease, and Pass the Slip Stitch Over (PSSO) a left-facing decrease.

Decreasing — Knit Two Together
Knit Two Together (K2TOG) is simply putting your needles through two loops rather than one.

For a knit stitch, the needle will go through two loops, starting with the loop to the left of the next stitch, and then through the next stitch, before picking up the yarn feed and pulling it through both loops, and then off the left needle.

Purl Two Together (P2TOG) feels easier, because the needle travels through the loop from right to left. The needle goes through two loops before picking up the yarn feed; pull it through just like a regular purl stitch.

Decreasing — Pass the Slip Stitch Over
Pass the Slip Stitch Over (PSSO) slips a stitch, knits the next stitch, then passes the slipped stitch over the knitted stitch and over the tip of the right needle (similar to casting off).

When purling, slip a stitch and purl the next stitch, then take the slipped stitch and pass it over the purled stitch and over the tip of the right needle (again, like casting off, purl-wise).

Decreasing — Triple Decreases

Some patterns ask for a triple decrease, that is, turning three stitches into one. Ann felt that knitting three together (K3TOG) was awkward. Her solution to the challenge of a triple decrease was as follows:

Slip one, knit two together, pass the slip stitch over (S1, K2 TOG, PSSO).

Breaking it into bite-sized pieces, as above, gives the same end result as K3TOG. Similarly, a triple decrease in purl stitch — purl three together (P3TOG) — can be achieved by breaking it down into smaller bits:

Slip one, purl two together, pass slip stitch over (S1, P2TOG, PSSO).

Stay Away from the Edge

One of Ann's cardinal rules was always to increase or decrease two stitches in from the edge so the increase or decrease blends in with the fabric. Increasing or decreasing in the first or last stitch in a row produces a bump that juts out along the edge of your knitting and is a "pain in the patootie" when sewing a seam.

Techniques Can Be Interchangeable (Sometimes)

To Ann, the written word was not sacrosanct. When a pattern called for one type of decrease, she encouraged us to exercise our options and substitute one technique for another. She only cautioned to be consistent, because each type of decrease has its own look; inconsistency will show.

On the other hand, the different increasing techniques have quite different looks, from solid to lacey. Ann warned that they are not as interchangeable as the decreasing techniques without altering the look of the finished product.

10

Yarn

ANN'S CLASS gave her an outlet for sharing with others, yet knitting was no mere excuse to connect. Knitting was a true passion for her, and the medium was very much a part of the message.

What is it about yarn, those twisted bits of fiber? Yarns are unparalleled transmitters of a host of so-called feminine traits: love, warmth, nurturing; no fiber-optic cable could send a clearer signal. Yarn speaks volumes, whether whispering a lullaby in a baby blanket, or packing an ironic punch in a "yarn-bombed" city bus.

A big part of Ann's charm derived from the lively contrast between her tough exterior and the tender art she practiced. A unique combination of hard and soft, she defied easy categorization.

To Ann, all ideas were to be questioned and considered and then selected, modified, or debunked on their merits. She was open to anything her intelligence recommended, and her curiosity led her down some idiosyncratic paths. Ann was deep into homeopathic remedies years before their current level of acceptance. She was also among the earliest to adopt a child from another country. So far ahead of the curve was Ann that she was mentioned in a *Ms. Magazine* article exploring the advance that she championed ("Should You Adopt a Foreign Baby?" *Ms. Magazine*, January 1983).

Yet Ann was far from New Age-y. She did not teach life lessons, per se. Her wisdom was all applied. The lessons had to be teased out from the fabric of her actions.

Here are the philosophical underpinnings of Ann's actions: independence of thought, pride in achievement, confidence in her judgment, commitment to the value of her contribution, and last but not least, devotion to her students. Whoever showed up — teen, disabled, senior, or housewife — was a welcome recipient of Ann's teaching. She did not keep her gifts to herself. She shared where she could, confident that the right people would be there to receive her message. And we were.

When you think about it, it shows a lot of faith. Somehow, the tough lady conveyed the most tender of values.

Yarn Weights

Most yarn comes in standard weights or thicknesses — worsted weight: five stitches per inch; heavyweight (also called bulky and super-bulky yarns): three or four stitches per inch; and light or fingering weight (includes sock yarn and baby yarns): seven or eight stitches per inch.

Sock yarn has 25 percent nylon added for strength and durability. Baby yarn comes in a variety of synthetic and natural fibers, and may have a bit more variation in gauge (stitches per inch).

Most commercial patterns specify the exact type of yarn and number of skeins needed. It makes sense, as subtle variations in fiber and texture — even within a standard weight — can affect your project.

Ann was not one to be ruled by a label. She declared sock and baby yarns to be interchangeable. No need to buy baby yarn to make a baby blanket. In fact, she favored sock yarn for baby projects, as it is generally packaged with more yards per skein than baby yarn, and offers more durability because of the added nylon or acrylic.

Your work is worth quality ingredients.

"BEWARE OF CRAPOLA!" warned Ann.

Never buy cheap yarn!
Inexpensive?
Yes!
Sale?
Great!
Cheap?
No!
Your work is worth quality ingredients.

NOT TO SAY that every project needs cashmere, or even wool. On the contrary, Ann understood that 100 percent acrylic makes the best choice for some projects.

Price is not always an indication of quality. Dinah once mail-ordered a quantity of expensive wool for a baby blanket. As she knit, the yarn just kept stretching and stretching. Finally, Ann suggested that Dinah return it, even though the yarn had been used. As per the manufacturer's instructions, Dinah simply rewound the yarn into a ball and sent it back for a full refund.

Beware of Crapola! (Part II)

To quote Ann, "Beware of chenille, beware of fun fur, beware of anything that looks like it has grown a hair coat!"

Her rule of thumb:
Let your skill shine through. Use plain, smooth, single-color, light- or medium-hued yarn to highlight your work to its best advantage.

And vice versa (if you must):

The more exotic the yarn (fun fur, ribbons, metallic, nubbly texture, multicolor, etc.), the more simple the pattern should be.

Wool and Superwash Wool
Some people find wool too itchy to wear, with good reason. Wool has microscopic thorn-like protrusions all along the fibers. (These protrusions are the reason wool has the ability to be felted: the little thorns grab each other and interlock.) Superwash wool is a product in which the thorns have been removed by a washing process, recommended for baby blankets and garments, and for anyone who is allergic to wearing wool.

Trust Your Senses
Ann's useful advice when buying yarn: Feel it! Rub it on your neck or on the back of your hand. Trust your own senses: If it doesn't feel good, don't buy it!

One Project, One Dye Lot
To match yarn for a project, you not only need the same fiber, brand, weight, and color, but also the same dye lot. Matching the dye lot — information given on the label — is the only way to be sure of matching the yarn. Purchase in advance the correct amount of yarn needed for a project. Run out of yarn and it may be near impossible to find a match.

Where Do These Yarns Come From?
Wool is from sheep.

Cashmere and mohair are from goats.

Alpaca is from alpacas.

Angora is from rabbits.

Silk is from silkworm cocoons.

Fiber Removal
Wool is removed from sheep by shearing. The sheep suffers no harm other than the indignity of being shorn. The sheep's crew cut is actually more comfortable in the hot summer months.

Love the winter woolens — hate bikini weather!

Angora is removed from angora rabbits by brushing or clipping. Ann had observed an angora rabbit being brushed. She reported that the rabbit was positively "orgasmic" ("If you saw the look on that rabbit's face…")!

Mmmm . . . a little to the left!

Plant-Based Fibers

Cotton is from the seedpod, or cotton boll on the cotton plant. Flax, also known as linen, is taken from the outer layer (the bast) of the stem of the flax plant. There are ever more plant-based yarns available, such as soy and bamboo.

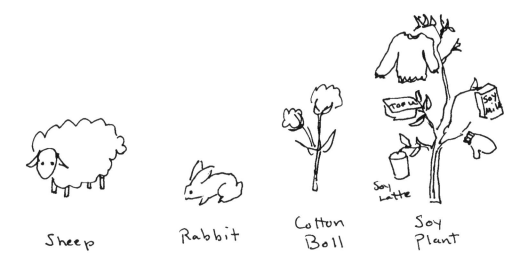

Sheep   Rabbit   Cotton
                               Boll   Soy
                                             Plant

Yarn fibers and their sources

The Fire Test for Unlabeled Yarn

Ann's method to test unlabeled yarn for content was to gently touch a match flame to a small end of yarn. Of course, do this in a safe place and take all safety precautions: Do the test far from any flammable materials, such as on a plate or metal dish, or in a sink.

Wool: smolders
Nylon: melts
Acrylic: flashes
Silk: stinks (similar to burning human hair)

Mohair

Ann said, "Do not bother with 50 percent mohair/50 percent acrylic. If you want mohair, use 100 percent or 90 percent mohair — that is, pure mohair. It's soft, light, easy to work with, and gorgeous."

Yarn Quantities

Yarn quantities vary widely according to brand and yarn type. To keep things interesting, some brands list quantity in yards, others in meters, and still others in weight, either ounces or grams.

Following are Ann's guidelines for yarn quantities for various projects, based on a skein of worsted-weight yarn. A good model would be one of her go-to favorites, Patons Canadiana, which holds approximately 241 yards (220 meters) per skein.

Hat: 1 skein
Scarf: 3 skeins
Sweater: 10-12 skeins
Baby afghan: 6 skeins
Afghan: 10-12 skeins
Bedspread: 14 skeins

Yarn Memory

Memory refers to the ability of the yarn to spring back into shape after stretching or washing. Wool fibers are naturally curly and interlocking, and that gives great bounce-back to anything knit from wool.

Cotton, alpaca, and silk do not have memory. Stretch it and it stays stretched. Ann did not recommend making garments out of these yarns. (They are fine for flat items.) If you wish to do so, Ann suggested using a cable or rib stitch to build some spring into the garment. She also noted that cabled cotton yarn, in which the threads are cabled together rather than twisted or spun, holds its shape better than twisted cotton yarn.

Nowadays, most commercial cotton garments have added spandex to help them keep their shape. Likewise, for knitted cotton garments, Ann recommended using 50 percent cotton/50 percent acrylic yarn.

11

A Break in the Yarn

SADLY, ANN passed away suddenly in June 2010. Her loss is keenly felt. Our group still meets and we regularly ask: "What would Ann do?"

As I look back, I am astonished at the sheer volume of information she passed to us in what was barely nine months' time. Virtually *all* the information in this book is from that brief period.

Losing anyone can be shocking, yet the strength of my feelings surprised even me. Ann shared her time, knowledge, resources, and encouragement, her stories and her friendship. Her loss made me fully recognize the generosity that guided her actions. Her teaching created a meeting ground, a bridge to others. Ann needed to share, and we needed what she offered.

FROM ALL APPEARANCES, Ann had passed away peacefully in her sleep. It was without warning, and we were all completely stunned.

I still find it hard to believe that it was our little group that discovered Ann's passing, but that is how it happened. The driver that Ann and Dinah shared called Dinah to say Ann was not waiting downstairs as she usually was, nor was she reachable by phone. Dinah called me. I told her to call the police. The police climbed in through the bedroom window, and that was how Ann was found.

I mention these details only to say that we had the somber privilege to be present, and even play a small part, at an important moment. Brief as our acquaintance was, there were strong ties binding Ann and our little group. We mattered to each other in ways that we may never fully understand.

Part of Ann's genius was her self-confidence; she so strongly believed in her concept of herself as a teacher. She did not run after accolades or put stock in outward measures of success. Her students weren't *just* high school kids, or *just* a free knitting class at the Y; each situation was exactly where she was meant to be, sharing her important, valuable knowledge with other important, valuable human beings. She would never have articulated it that way, but she lived and breathed that confidence, strength, independence, and generosity. May the thread of Ann's teaching continue unbroken, and may her life be an inspiration and encouragement to all those who have a passion to learn or a passion to share.

Her students weren't just high school kids, or just a free knitting class at the Y; each situation was exactly where she was meant to be, sharing her important, valuable knowledge with other important, valuable human beings.

12

Ann's Notions & Knitting Bags

ANN WAS A LOVING SCOLD. She had the inner conviction that if she could just set everyone straight, the world would be a better place.

And try she did, scolding mothers in the street to take the plastic covers off their baby carriages ("they need fresh air!"), and gently ribbing (pun intended) her students into knitting success. Some folks didn't appreciate her style, but those who did wanted more of whatever she was giving out.

Ann's tips are all designed to help you "do it smarter." Her tips on what to carry in your knitting bag are no different:

Do it smarter — do it Ann's way! — and make life just plain better.

Each Project Gets Its Own Bag

If you have more than one knitting project going (a "must," per Ann), each project gets its own knitting bag.

She recommended LeSportsac bags. They are light, strong, well-made, and they zipper shut. Ann liked the kind with a gusset so the bag doesn't flop over when you set it down.

Do it smarter — do it Ann's way! — and make life just plain better.

IPod   IPad   IKnit

73

Knitting Notions

Ann kept a notions kit in each project bag, along with the project itself (the yarn and needles in a Ziploc bag, of course).

She liked using clear plastic make-up bags for her knitting notions.

Following is Ann's extensive list of handy items that might be useful when working on a project. I've broken it into two parts:

Useful Knitting Tools:

1. Tape measure

2. Stitch markers

3. Crochet hook — size G

4. Tapestry needles

5. Point holders or rubber bands, to protect knitting needle tips and prevent your knitting from slipping off the needle

6. Small scissors: lightweight and blunt-nosed so as not to stick a hole in your bag; blunt-end kids' scissors work great

7. Needle gauge (aka needle-sizer), used to determine unmarked needle sizes. It is a piece of metal with holes punched in various sizes — stick your unlabelled needle in the right size hole to see what its size is

8. Cable stitch holder — smallest one, V-shaped

9. Stitch holders — big safety pins work great

10. Size 2 double-pointed needles to pick up dropped stitches (always use a smaller-size needle for knitting fixes)

11. 24-inch circular needle

Accessories Ann liked to keep close at hand when knitting:

1. Emory board — for hangnails, so they don't get caught in the yarn (ouch!)

2. Band-Aids — to protect any small cuts on your hands from being irritated by yarn

3. Wipe-ups — to clean your hands and knitting needles

4. Small notebook and pen — invaluable

5. Ziploc bags

AS I LEARN MORE about Ann in the course of writing, I see unsuspected parallels with my own family. A shared fascination with yarn and knitting is one such parallel. Only after embarking on this project did I discover that my sister had also taken up knitting. Not only did we unexpectedly share an interest, but that interest came into both our lives at a similar moment. What are the chances?

My mother was a serious painter and sculptor. Though a talented knitter and crocheter since her childhood, in mid-life she took up hook rugs with a passion; the hooked rugs married her artistic love of color and pattern with that cozy, embracing, nurturing medium: yarn. So, the women in my family seem to be drawn to yarn; does a common longing drive this shared attraction?

Having coffee with Ann's daughter, Michelle, I discovered that Ann was a bit of a pack rat. This piece of information stunned me with recognition that hit close to home: My mother also shared that tendency. It was beginning to feel like more than mere coincidence.

I see Ann and my mother as immensely talented, independent women, both of whom bucked convention as they charted their own course in life. What drove those maverick choices? Did they hold in common some mysterious equation whereby their unconventionality and independence were counterbalanced and soothed by the comfort offered by fiber arts and objects?

ABOUT A YEAR INTO WRITING — after I had loosely organized my knitting notes into book form — I developed a strange aversion to the task I had set for myself. I could not go on. In retrospect, my writer's block seemed to stem from an inner reluctance to go where my material was leading me, a refusal to look it square in the face. When I finally gathered my courage to face my demons, I found an opening that allowed me to continue the project, but in a surprising new direction.

As I mulled over the possible causes of my project fatigue, I stumbled on a connection with my own past. In its original form the book too closely echoed my childhood preoccupation with my adored mother, whose depression and unhappy marriage took her away from me. If I could just get her on her feet, my six-year-old self reasoned, then perhaps she could turn around and give me the nurturing I needed. My mission, then, became to make her happy. So I studied her, supported her, cheered her up, and cheered her on. It was a full-time job, and, as may be guessed, not one destined for success.

I resolved to do with this book what I could not fully do back then: to share more of myself in the story. This was my first inkling that the book was to be substantially different than all my other unfinished projects. I felt more than a bit alarmed: Could I bring my own story to this tale? If I wanted to continue, I had to; otherwise, it seemed, my writing genie was going on strike and this project would join the pile in the drawer.

As soon as I made that resolution, the fatigue lifted and the writing flowed. My answer — to share more of myself — felt scary, but right.

I had no idea where this was going when I began taking notes in Ann's class. Yet this new direction felt inevitable, squirm though I may. There are things that want to be said, even if they are said (strange world!) in the midst of a knitting book. I would not have chosen to expose this childhood grief, nor do I wish to reflect badly on my beloved mother, yet I am determined to obey my inner voice, to follow the yarn started so many months ago in Ann's class.

To my eternal surprise, this project somehow affords me a chance to achieve a balance it was not in my power to achieve as a child, and I am deeply grateful for that second chance. My goal became to honor and memorialize Ann and share her treasure trove of information, and at the same time to try to fulfill my own need to be seen and heard. Thankfully, the recognition and acceptance I felt in Ann's class sustains me. It continues to be the informing spirit of this project, and it encourages me to claim a share of the space on these pages for a bit of my own story alongside Ann's.

The point of the exercise changed. Like an improvised sweater, new events and insights shape the garment as it grows. Slowly, the threads of Ann's life and mine, of her family and mine, of her story and mine, begin to be knit together.

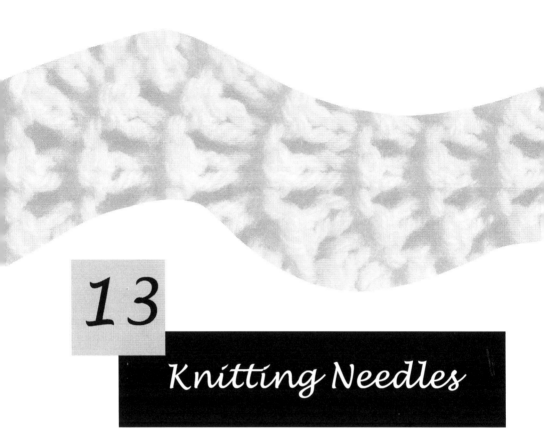

13

Knitting Needles

Addi Turbo Knitting Needles

To Ann, Addi Turbos were the *ne plus ultra* of knitting needles. They are stainless steel and offer frictionless action any serious knitter will appreciate.

Bamboo Knitting Needles

In one of her characteristically practical observations, Ann noted that bamboo knitting needles do not retain heat, which makes them comfortable in even the hottest weather. They grab yarn more than metal needles, an asset when working with slippery yarn or using double-pointed needles.

Her trick for cleaning bamboo needles was to plunge them in and out of dry rice a few times, or rub them gently with very fine steel wool.

Circular Knitting Needles

Circular needles are attached at both ends of a plastic wire. The needles are about five inches long and the wire is of varying length.

The transition from the wire to the needle should be smooth to allow the knitting to flow freely, otherwise the knitter has to stop every few stitches to nudge the yarn onto the needle — a real pain in the patootie. Addi Turbo makes a good circular needle; there are good bamboo circular needles as well. Heed Ann's advice: Spend the extra cash on good circular needles or you will have a frustrating time of it.

Circular needles may be used to knit flat pieces or to knit in the round. A 24-inch circular needle is handy for sleeves, collars, scarves, hats, and more. Long wires (Ann suggested 60 inches) allow you to do big projects, like afghans, that you couldn't comfortably hold on regular needles.

Projects don't fall off circular needles as easily as they might with regular needles. When I store

In one of her characteristically practical observations, Ann noted that bamboo knitting needles do not retain heat, which makes them comfortable in even the hottest weather.

79

my projects, I tie the two needles together, effectively locking the project on the wire.

Circular needles come with the wire curled up in its packaging. To relax the curl and make them easier to use, Ann recommended soaking new needles in warm water. If you are using bamboo circular needles, do not wet the bamboo part, just soak the wire.

14

Loose Ends

WHEN ANN WAS STILL ALIVE, I had no idea that this book would take such a personal turn, or that I would find so many connections to my heart and to my past. I simply liked being in class, and I was grateful for the immense gift of knowledge Ann shared with us.

Chaya, Dinah, and I took Ann out to lunch two weeks before she passed away. It was our way of saying thank you. In retrospect, we were so grateful that we did the lunch and did not put it off for another time. As small a gesture as it was, Ann knew we appreciated her.

I take it as yet another lesson from Ann: In life, as in knitting, don't leave loose ends. Take the time to thank the people who matter in your life.

SEWING A SEAM, tucking in loose ends, all are part of the fine art of finishing your work. The impact on your garment of good finishing versus bad finishing can mean the difference between Ann's definitions of handmade and homemade. One — handmade (skilled craftsmanship) — is to be treasured; the other — homemade (uneven execution) — is not up to snuff in Ann's book.

"*Handmade* is not *homemade*. Do it right and wear it with pride!"

Ann would never allow any aspect of a project to betray her hard work or high intentions. Just as she regarded washing knitted garments as an extension of her knitting, so too she insisted upon completing every aspect of a project with finesse.

Shortcuts and clever solutions were terrific, as long as the result was handmade rather than homemade.

> *Take the time to thank the people who matter in your life.*

No Knots!

In Ann's immortal words: "Etch this on your eyelids: Never, ever, ever, ever, ever knot your yarn!"

To Ann, Murphy's Law would dictate that a knot, carefully tucked into the back of a knitted garment, will invariably pull to the front of the garment upon washing, or will unknot itself and ruin the garment, something Ann would label a "real pain in the patootie!"

Attaching a New Ball of Yarn: No Knots!

Overlap the tail end of the old yarn (pointing left) and the start end of the new yarn (pointing right) in your yarn feed hold. Knit both yarns together for about one inch.

In Skeins of Wool: No Knots!

If you find a knot in a skein of wool (yes, it happens): Unknot or cut the knot out and treat the two ends as if you were attaching a new ball of yarn, as above.

No Knots! No Knots! No Knots!

Ann's no-knots policy held true of commercial products as well. As sharp a shopper as she was a savvy knitter, she encouraged us to inspect (and reject) for knots when shopping.

Attach New Yarn As Far From Center Stage As Possible

Minimize any visual disturbance in the center of the work; at the edges, a join will more likely escape notice.

Twist Yarns Together When Attaching New Yarn

When joining two strands of yarn, twist them together. In effect, this spins the two yarns together, and will help secure the yarn: A twisted yarn is less likely to slip out and unravel.

This will help prevent a mistake I experienced firsthand when my yarns were not twisted together. I saw what appeared to be two loops on my needle; I knit each loop separately, thereby doubling the number of stitches. Big mistake! The twist helps identify the two yarns as one loop, helping the knitter stay on pattern.

Splicing Yarn

Splicing effectively hand spins together two yarns. There are no ends to bury, so it avoids the bulk of double yarn. Done well, it should be virtually invisible.

Unwind the yarn ply (the different strands that make up the yarn) at both ends. Trim the plies to varying lengths. Feed the ends into each other so they overlap, and hand twist the yarn back together so the two ends grab each other. This technique works best on three- or more-ply yarn.

Burying the Yarn

Hanging tails of yarn need to be taken care of by burying the yarn. (Tails result when casting on or off or when joining new yarn.)

84

Use a needlepoint needle to thread the tail up on the wrong side of the garment for three to four inches. Where possible, Ann threaded the tail through the loops of the purl stitch — "this way, you'll never find it!"

If there are two loose ends near each other, Ann would bury one end going one way and the other end going the other way, so as not to create too much bulk in one area. Bury about four inches worth of yarn; any remaining length can be snipped off after you have buried it.

A crochet hook is also useful for burying yarn. Ann advised using the smallest hook possible so as not to stretch the knit loops. (The goal is to hide the yarn end, not call unwanted attention to the area by stretching out the stitches!)

I confess: One of my least favorite tasks is burying yarn, so I cheat where possible: I knit my cast-on tail into the first row of stitches. I just knit the tail (twisted along with my yarn) for about six or seven stitches and snip the rest. The same trick works for attaching a new ball of yarn. I knit enough to secure it (again six or seven stitches), and snip the rest. Yay!

15

Tying Up a Loose End for Ann

OUR GROUP HAD THE PRIVILEGE to tie up a loose end for Ann. I recalled that she had been working on a blanket during class and I offered her daughter, Michelle, help finishing the project. Michelle told me that, among Ann's belongings, she had found a quantity of knitted squares that were obviously intended for an afghan. Chaya, Dinah, and I arranged to meet Michelle for the first time. Michelle brought the squares. Although this was clearly not the blanket I remembered Ann working on in class (described in detail in the chapter on Ann's Knit Projects), I was delighted to help.

Chaya, Dinah, and Michelle — Team Afghan: a fuzzy cell phone photo, and a dear memento.
Though not present at this first meeting, Anoush is also part of the team.

Why was I so eager to take on another task? Knitting in general offers a sense of accomplishment: Projects are finite and, for the most part, achievable. Unlike so much in life the product is tangible; you can hold it in your hands, even snuggle up in it. This was a task I could complete!

Once again, the connection to Ann resonated in my own life. Perhaps this was something I could do for Ann that I could not do for my own parents. When it came to my own family, the tasks were either too daunting or they simply did not fall to me to do. My dad's third wife took charge of his care during his final illness; my sister was in charge of care for my mom. In both cases, I was a welcome visitor, yet no essential task was left for me to do. This was both a great blessing and a great loss. Each caretaker also took control of the narrative of the lives of their loved one, protecting it from other voices; in this, too, I felt at a strange distance from the immediacy of my personal connection to the events.

Tying up one loose end for Ann helped me tie up a lifetime of loose ends of my own.

How had it come to this? I had been trained to be *nice*, which meant to suppress my needs and provide space for the needs of others. My parents divorced when I was six and the conflict continued until a court battle gave my father custody seven years later. To survive, I imagined I was a princess whose restraint would surely be recognized and rewarded. The problem is, I was the only one in on my silent Cinderella strategy. To others, I must have seemed content to play a supporting role. My behavior only perpetuated the pattern, habituating me not to speak up and not to have my needs met, and habituating those around me not to consider my needs.

The deaths of my parents forced me to confront my role in my family, and it is not a pretty picture. So many of my adult choices finally began to make sense: I had re-created my childhood reality over and over again. What has made it so difficult to untangle is that the pattern had been wrapped in a fabrication about a happy family and a daughter who should have no complaints.

Amazing grace, Ann came into my life and provided the key to unknot this childhood trauma that had continued to shape my experience well into adulthood. Without ever making any fuss about it, her naturally respectful treatment of me grounded me in truth and righteousness, returned me my dignity, and gave me a steady measure by which to assess other behavior.

When I started writing this book, I was mystified by how touched I was by Ann. After all, we were not that close, and I had not studied with her for that long, so why did this tough-talking woman move me to tears? I know now it is because she gave me the rare and precious gifts of trust, respect, and freedom.

The acceptance I received from Ann was a healing miracle. By some quirky cosmic alchemy, this brief encounter transformed my entire experience; tying up one loose end for Ann helped me tie up a lifetime of loose ends of my own. No longer blindly knitting stitch after stitch, living unaware, working on the reverse side of the fabric, suddenly, awareness lifted me above my actions, and a glimpse of the grand design was revealed.

It is good to be able to set down my experience here uninterrupted and uncensored. The heartache I felt around my parents' passing went some ways toward being healed when Ann entrusted me with her story, and again when Ann's daughter not only allowed me to share her mother's story, but also accepted my vision of her mother's story as an avenue to explore my own truth.

Granted, finishing a blanket or writing a book in no way compensates the pain of a childhood trauma. And, true, doing for someone outside one's own family is often easier than doing for one's own kin. Yet somehow, with this book and with Ann's blanket, I could heal my loss a little bit. I could grieve a passing parent. I could jump in and be useful. I can reclaim my space. I can tell my story.

FINISHING A LARGE PROJECT can be daunting, so with invaluable aesthetic input from Chaya and Dinah, and crocheting help from Anoush and Chaya, we got to work assembling the afghan. We were privileged to be able to do this work in Ann's memory, and, a short time later, to be able to deliver an object that was both a gift from her own hands, and at the same time a token of our gratitude to her, to Ann's daughter, Michelle.

The afghan that Anoush, Chaya, Dinah, and I completed
for Michelle, with squares knit by Ann

16

Inheriting the Yarn

A FEW MONTHS into the class, when that pesky voice in my head that said, "I want to write about Ann," refused to go away, I took the plunge and told Ann I wanted to write about her. When she responded, "Sure," I knew I was in deep water.

While Ann was alive I had done no more than take notes; I had assumed I would have the benefit of her guidance on this project. With an original working title of *Knit Wit* ("We'll see," said Ann, sagely, skeptically), I envisioned the book as a loose collection of knitting notes and quotable Ann-isms. When Ann passed away, our agreement took on a new meaning, and in that instant the project changed radically.

By default, I inherited Ann's mandate to share the information she had so painstakingly amassed. I could no longer back out. If I didn't want to sink, I had better start to swim, and so I began transforming my notes into this book. It has been quite a journey.

I like to imagine that it meant something to Ann to know her teachings would be passed on. I have a persistent notion that it might even have been something she had been waiting for, something she needed to have in place before she could depart. Her trust in me — to leave me with the task yet undone — is awesome, and humbling. I hope this book helps fulfill Ann's deep desire — her mission, really — to share her knowledge with others.

Ann's sense of urgency, too, passed to me. Without the ghost of her at my elbow, whispering in my ear, "I'm counting on you," I would not have been able to swim to shore and carry this project through to completion.

I like to imagine that it meant something to Ann to know her teachings would be passed on.

17

Joining Knit Pieces

WHILE MANY KNITTERS are fanatical about knitting, some may not feel quite the same passion for sewing. One option is to avoid seams where possible. Ann described a patchwork afghan she knit that was pieced together by her seamstress mother; this sweet solution did double duty to produce both a meaningful family heirloom and a neat answer to the challenge of seam work.

However, avoidance has its limits and sometimes a seam must be sewn. Here are Ann's thoughts on joining knit pieces.

Use the Tail as Your Joining Thread

Using the yarn tail as the thread for seam work was one of Ann's cleverest ideas. She liked that the seam is integral to the piece, which is always stronger than adding new yarn. Furthermore, and I love this part, there are fewer ends to bury. This works equally well using a cast-on tail or a cast-off tail. For a sewn seam, leave a tail about two times the length of the seam. A knitted or crocheted seam uses more yarn; allow 1.5 inches of yarn per stitch.

Needlework Joining: Ladder Stitch

A basic ladder stitch will serve most situations. It is done with right sides facing, using a large embroidery needle. The needle, threaded with the same yarn as your garment, goes under the bar at the bottom of the first stitch, then through the same position on the second piece, back and forth, up the garment stitch by stitch until the seam is sewn.

Try to match stitches row for row, or the seam will pucker. Ann's rule of good edges creates a selvage that has half the number of loops as there are rows, making a consistent, easy-to-read edge for seaming.

Pin the seam to help keep the two sides in tandem as you sew. I have found that even when I am paying ferocious attention, one side tends to

Sometimes a seam must be sewn.

99

stretch more than the other as I sew; nothing is as disheartening as discovering a length of extra fabric on one side at the end of a (tedious!) seam. A few well-spaced pins help keep the seam on track and minimize the amount of redoing or fudging you may need at the end. Pinning is useful for crocheted and knitted seams as well.

Needlework Joining: Whip Stitch
For seam work that is part of the design, Ann liked a whip stitch in the same or contrasting color to the knit work.

Needlework Joining: Grafting
"Grafting is like knitting with a sewing needle," useful for invisible joins. Sadly, it is one of several tantalizing techniques that Ann did not get to teach our class. I mention it as something to be aware of and perhaps pursue further.

Knitted Joining: Three-Needle Bind-Off
The three-needle bind-off is stronger than grafting and useful for sleeve and shoulder seams. If you prefer knitting to sewing, it is a good way to dispense with a few seams without picking up a sewing needle.

For a shoulder seam, for example, have both shoulders on knitting needles. Hold both pieces parallel, both needles pointed the same way, both pieces right side in. With a third needle, go through the first loop on both needles before you pull the yarn through. Knit the second stitch the same way. Slip the first stitch over the second stitch, as you normally would in order to bind off. Continue in the same way until you have cast off the entire seam.

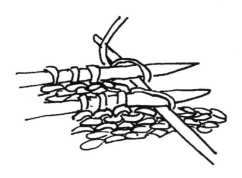

Three-needle bind-off

The third needle should be smaller than the project's needles so as not to overstretch the stitches. On the other hand, to allow more give in the seam, use a needle two sizes bigger as your third needle.

Crocheted Joining

To crochet join a knit garment, simply use the holes in the knit fabric as if they were the previous row of crochet, that is, use your hook as you usually would. The skill is in spacing the stitches correctly; there may not be a one-for-one correspondence between the knit stitches and the crochet stitches.

Picking Up Stitches: Adding Knitting to a Knit Fabric

Adding knitting to knit fabric, such as knitting a collar on a sweater, calls for picking up stitches. Assuming the body of the sweater has already been cast off, simply use a knitting needle to enter a (cast off) stitch and pull through a loop from your yarn feed. Repeat for as many stitches as you need to pick up, traveling along the edge, adding loops to your needle. Knit the loops as you normally would.

Patterns will specify, for example, "Pick up 100 stitches evenly spaced around the collar." Use quilter's pins to mark off quadrants along the collar: 25 loops are easier to space correctly than 100 loops, and easier to redo as well, if need be.

Adding Knitting to a Fabric Garment

To add knitting to fabric, such as a knitted cuff or ruffle, use yarn to sew a buttonhole stitch along the edge of the fabric. Use a knitting needle to pick up stitches (as above) through the loops of the buttonhole stitches. Carry on knitting with two needles after that.

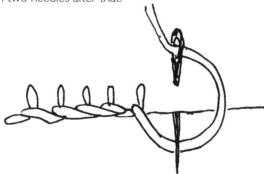

Buttonhole stitch along the edge of fabric: Use the loops to pick up stitches and start your knitting.

MY PROMISE to Ann was a commitment I could not neglect. In truth, the task has given me great gifts.

I have been one of those people sadly afflicted with the disease of *ending-itis*. Like the worst kind of spoiler, or, let's be honest, just plain afraid, I want to know in advance: Who will want to read this book? What kind of book will it be? Will anyone be interested? Dare I be an author of (of all things) a knitting book? Why am I doing this? and Who cares?

Maybe the answer to all those questions is not to entertain them at all. Demographics and target marketing are well and good, but sometimes one cannot know the answers in advance.

I finally understood that if I knew the ending in advance, the story might not be worth following. So I learned what every child already knows: You cannot pick the flowers without taking the walk. The gifts were hidden in the writing of the book. They can only be released by doing the task. The doing and the daring are the magic keys to unlocking the treasure chest.

IF I HAD NOT WRITTEN the book, I would not have turned to my friends to read it. If I had not turned to my friends, I would not have received their wisdom and their confidence in my voice. If I had not received their confidence in my voice, I would never have believed in myself as an author. If I had not believed in myself as an author, I would not be here, right now, with you. Thank you for sharing my journey.

Learning to follow the yarn has been the biggest gift of all. It is the lesson least expected and yet the one most needed as I catch myself in my daily life, straining for result rather than experience on matters big and small: Will I make the next traffic light? Will I win the next game? Will this relationship work out?

I have to remind myself to stop, stop seeking the end of the yarn! There is nothing at the end of the yarn. Enjoy the journey, play the game, live the relationship. It has been a loosening of control — control over things I could not control anyway, control that only hindered, not helped, the outcome.

Ann provided the spark that started this process. I am grateful to her for her confidence in my ability to present her teachings in my words, through the prism of my experience. Thank you, Ann.

18

General Tips & Tools

Have More than One Project Going

Ann advocated having more than one project going at a time. Tackle different projects as the mood strikes you, take breaks, and return to a project refreshed. Work on heavier projects in the winter and lighter ones in the summer.

Summer knitting   *Winter knitting*
                        (Circular needles come in handy!)

Save smaller projects for commutes, bigger ones for home. Commuter projects should use smaller needles so as not to stab your neighbors — unless, of course, you purposely choose long needles with self-defense in mind (perfect for forays through dicey neighborhoods!).

Defensive knitting

Index Cards

Ann liked putting patterns on index cards, one row of the pattern per card, clipped together on a ring so they stay in order and flip easily. Flip the cards as you knit and avoid the headache of searching for your place in a pattern.

Plastic Sleeves

She also suggested making an extra copy of any pattern you use. Store the original in plastic sleeves (she collected binders full of patterns), and keep the copy you are using protected in a plastic sleeve(s) as well.

Quilter's Pins

Quilter's pins are big safety pins. Ann used them when pinning to take measurements and when calculating a pattern. She liked to store quilter's pins in an old Band-Aid box (I love this retro idea, if you can find an old tin anymore).

Stitch Markers (aka Dots)

Stitch markers provide visual cues that allow the knitter to ease up on counting. They make knitting much easier, and they are easy to use: Just pass them from one needle to the other when you get to them.

For Feather and Fan stitch, where each repeat in the pattern is 18 stitches long, Ann had us place a dot in between each repeat. If something was off, it would be obvious by the time you reached your dot — undoing 18 stitches is a lot easier than ripping out rows of work.

Ann felt rubber dots were easier to control than hard plastic ones. They are flexible enough that they don't pop off as you move them. Some knitters enjoy fancy stitch markers decorated with beads and such; making and collecting them can be a hobby in itself.

Ann suggested using different color dots or double dots to signal different sections of work. For example, use one color in between each pattern repeat, and another color to indicate a border. The dots allow you to go on automatic until you get your wake-up call when you reach the border.

Stitch Holders

A stitch holder is like a giant safety pin. It is used to hold stitches off the needles if, say, you are holding loops from the back of a collar, or if you need to borrow your knitting needles from one project to another. Just slip stitches onto the holder, then slip them back on the needle when you are ready to continue knitting.

Stitch holder

Ann's Innovative Use for a Stitch Holder

Ann used a stitch holder to hold a scarf in a neat bundle while knitting it. Use the largest size — which is about 5-6 inches across. Just roll up your scarf and pin it together "so it doesn't trail all over the place as you knit, which is a pain in the patootie!"

Option A: Mop the floor.

Option B: Hang 'em high.

Option C: Pardon my scarf.

Option D: Use a stitch holder!

Double Yarn

Double yarn is simply knitting with two strands of yarn as if they were one. Ann thought it helpful to wind the two yarns together into a single ball of yarn.

Knit Lace

For lacey stitches, Ann recommended going up two needle sizes more than what is asked for in the pattern, to allow the holes to show to best effect.

Yarn Separator

For Fair Isle knitting, which uses multiple colors. The yarn separator helps keep the different yarns apart and untangled.

Cable Holders

A cable holder is a double-pointed needle with a little dip in the middle, used to hold a bit of knitting to the side when making a cable. The dip makes it harder for your stitches to accidentally slip off.

A double-pointed needle (DPN) can be used instead of a cable holder. Bamboo works particularly well, as it is less slippery than metal, which helps keep the loops from sliding off.

Ann recommended using a cable holder or DPN that is a size or two smaller than your project's needles, so as not to overstretch your stitches.

19

Fixes

ANN SAID: "NEVER BE AFRAID of tearing something out because that is where you learn. If you never make a mistake, there's something wrong with what you are doing!"

On the other hand, some mistakes are too insignificant to bear correcting. Ann quoted her mother: "Mistakes: A smart one won't tell; a dumb one won't notice."

Know the difference. Know which mistakes to tear out and redo, and which ones to let lie. Find the balance.

Rule #1
"When you are frustrated, put it down and walk away!"

IT IS UNCANNY how the knottiest problems are often solved in the simplest way. You can read a pattern nine times without penetrating the sense of it, while on the tenth reading everything becomes perfectly clear. Once a solution has been found, you can hardly understand how you didn't see it earlier. In fact, you can't even imagine not seeing something so obvious.

If Ann taught us anything, it is that sometimes you have to think outside the box. When Dinah was having the devil of a time trying to make a certain stitch come out right, Ann challenged her to keep trying. After several tries, Ann told her to see if perhaps the printed pattern contained an error, which — gasp! — indeed it did.

Pick your projects wisely, and pick your pattern-writers carefully. Go for it, keep trying, but don't always assume the mistake is yours.

Un-knitting Knitting
At times Ann mentioned topics that we somehow never got to, or I happened to miss that class. Un-knitting knitting was one of those. By dint of necessity I caught up. Basically, any knitter who ever makes an error (ha!) will have to undo a certain amount of work. If you do not wish to rip out your entire project, you may have to un-knit some stitches.

> "Mistakes: A smart one won't tell; a dumb one won't notice."

Ripping out whole rows is easy: Simply remove the needles and pull the yarn (i.e., unravel the work). When a finer approach is called for, un-knitting comes into play: Carefully knit in reverse, undoing your work stitch by stitch, until you find and correct your problem spot.

Un-knitting is intuitive. To learn more, I refer you to one of Ann's favorite sources: Barbara G. Walker's *Learn-to-Knit Afghan Book*.

Just one more row!
(Who said knitting was relaxing?!)

Use a Smaller Needle for Fixing Stitches
Always go smaller when doing fixes so as not to stretch stitches as you fiddle with them. Ann recommended carrying a size 2 double-pointed needle in your bag to use for any knit fixes.

Look at What You Are Doing
I saw this in my notes from Ann's class.

It sounds crazy obvious.

I mention it nonetheless.

Especially when making a complex pattern, it is tempting to follow the instructions blindly, as it were, and see the result only after the piece has taken shape. Ann encouraged us to do a bit more than that.

Really look at the work as you knit. Know the shape and feel of each stitch. This will help you see what presents, and make corrections if you have to un-knit something.

As Ann would say: "See where you are." You will recognize when something looks off, and you won't have to knit rows and rows before you notice a mistake.

Knit Leans Left, Purl Leans Right

It took me a while to understand Ann's cryptic statement: "Knit leans left, purl leans right." This tiny detail helps enormously when it comes to making fixes such as picking up a dropped stitch or un-knitting knitting.

If you look closely at knit fabric, knit and purl stitches are both flat to the front; in other words, the loops face front. Yet to hold the loops on a needle, they must rotate sideways, turned to profile, as it were. The knit loop is rotated leftward as it sits on the needle, the purl loop is rotated rightward on the needle.

Pilling

Pills are the little fuzz balls that stick to a garment and completely destroy its looks. Ann advised using a disposable razor blade to gently shave the pills off a garment. When the blade gets dull, throw it out and replace it with a new one. Another fix is using a nail scrub brush to gently brush the pills away.

Blocking

Blocking is drying or steam pressing the garment into a desired size and shape. Blocking won't turn a 6-inch wide scarf into an 9-inch wide scarf, but it can make a noticeable difference.

Wash the garment and dry flat on towels. When it is 90 percent dry, place the garment wrong side up on top of a towel on an ironing board. Cover with a tea towel. With a warm — not hot — iron, gently press down through the tea towel. Do not move the iron, just lift and press, lift and press. Use the steam setting, and let the steam do the work, rather than the pressure.

Some knitters use special blocking boards, and pins to hold the garment in shape as it dries. This is an area for further study, as Ann did not spend much class time on blocking.

When I made an afghan, I noticed that one of Ann's favorite authors, Barbara Walker, paid considerable attention to blocking the squares before assembling the afghan. Though Ann was a huge Walker fan, on this point she differed. Ann advised me to assemble the squares without blocking, explaining that the natural tension between the connected squares would effectively remedy any differences in square size. She was right.

Blocking and Zippered Sweaters

Ann advised against zippered sweaters because you cannot block them if need be. The fabric of the zipper has no give and won't allow it to be shaped in the same way that a knitted garment can be adjusted.

WHEN I LOOK BACK on Ann's class, I feel a sense of mystery. Our lives intersected. Our lives touched.

Dinah, a classmate who was new to our area, calls Ann her guardian angel — Ann's advice and friendship was that timely and meaningful. Chaya went from complete novice to now receiving requests from relatives for knitted garments. And here I am, writing a book about the experience, discovering ever new riches as I mine deeper. Astonishing.

I credit the strength of our feelings entirely to Ann. She had a gift of cutting through the boundaries that separate us and turning strangers into friends. It should come as no surprise that, over the years, Ann's driver, too, had become a friend. He was devoted to her, and she had stepped in to help his family at a crucial moment. Where someone else might have seen a label — *driver* or *student* — Ann saw a whole person.

When I went to Smiley's Yarns in Jamaica, Queens (Ann always talked about Smiley's Yarns), and mentioned to the manager, Raymond Stambouli, that I was writing about Ann, his eyes softened. "Of course I remember Ann," he said. After we chatted a bit, he confided, "You know, we had a special connection." (Why was I not surprised?) He told me that Ann had guided his family through their own adoption process.

The wonder of Ann is not simply that she knew so much and gave so generously. The miracle is that she somehow was able to uncover each person's need. Not only could she help with diverse issues, she could discover them in the first place — two highly different skills. Some say there are no accidents in life, that we share a common bond with the person sitting next to us on the bus, or the person behind the cash register. This may be true, but most of us never find out. We pass in anonymity, never knowing that perhaps we each hold the keys to unlock the other's challenges. Time and again, Ann did find out, and did something about it.

Raymond told me that once, when he was in the upstairs office, he happened to mention to Smiley's owner that Ann Sokolowski was in the store. Ann Sokolowski? The name rang a bell. Suddenly, he placed it: As a child he had suffered from a severe lisp, and had consulted with numerous doctors and speech therapists, all to no avail. After years of frustration, Ann came into his life when he was a teen (remember, she was a speech teacher) and, sure enough, cured him of his lisp. This had occurred at least four decades ago. Raymond and I looked at each other: Ann was amazing. As Raymond pointed out, you did not *have* to follow her advice — only if you wanted to "get it right!"

Next, Raymond introduced me to the two women at the register, Dorothy and Nalini. Again, I was regaled with anecdotes of how Ann would come in, sharing stories, homeopathic remedies, and gifts of peanut brittle, pumpkin butter, and prunes soaked in port wine ("really stewed prunes," they chuckled). It wasn't that Ann was friendly simply because this was a yarn store and she was a knitting maven. No, Ann had known Nalini for over 12 years; the relationship had begun when Nalini worked as cashier at Lewis of Woodhaven hardware store. Ann was Ann, yarn or no yarn. People were people, and Ann touched people's lives.

The recognition flowed both ways. I remember Ann telling us a story about her car. Her daughter, Michelle, filled in the details:

> It was the end of the school day and my mom was about to drive home. She said to herself, "Wow, the floor of my car is dirty." They were dirty because someone had stolen the leather seats out of her car. She got a milk crate from the school security guards and used that as a seat to drive across the street to a garage. It was the local don who owned the shop and my mom was giving his nephew speech lessons. She pulled up and I guess either the don recognized her or she said who she was, because the don said: "They did this? To your car? Wait here." Twenty minutes later she had brand new seats and the don said: "Don't worry Ms. Sokolowski, ain't nobody gonna touch your seats ever again."

You can bet Ann's car was never tampered with again.

20

Design Tips

Eye Happy, I Happy

Ann maintained that a sense of balance or symmetry keeps the eye happy, and vice versa, asymmetry disturbs the eye, whether the viewer is conscious of the cause or not.

Symmetry dictates an odd number of repeats in a row. A symmetrical pattern radiates out from a central point, so that one half of the fabric (folded lengthwise) is a mirror image of the other half.

Button Placement

Ann declared that buttons must be placed "mid-boobie" (i.e., in line with the widest part of the chest, usually at the nipples), not above or below, or the closure will gap, and "there is not a darn thing you can do about it and it will drive you up a wall."

Mind the gap!

No Buttons on Children's Sweaters

As Ann pointed out, anyone who has ever dressed a wriggling child will understand why she recommended no-button, V-neck sweaters for children.

Children Grow Up, Not Out!

Ann liked to quote her mother: "Children grow up, not out!" She advised knitting a sweater to fit a child without cuffs or ribbed bottom. As the child grows, add a few inches of cuffs and ribbing, so the child can get another year's wear out of it.

> ## "Children grow up, not out!"

Ann liked adding cuffs and ribs in a contrasting color. She liked combinations of bright primary colors — for example, a yellow sweater with red or blue cuffs and ribbing.

Adding cuffs and ribbing works especially well for sweaters knit from the neck down. Simply undo the bind off, and pick up where you left off to add length.

Of course, this can be taken to extremes:

Seriously, Mom, I think I just need a new sweater!

Knitting Needles for Hat Projects

For hats knitted in the round, Ann used 8-inch double-pointed needles, rather than circular needles. She felt that circular needles became too unwieldy when you have decreased down to, say, your final 12 stitches. She used four needles to hold the project and a fifth as the pick-up needle.

For a knitted cap with a ribbed cuff, Ann recommended making the ribbing with a needle one or two sizes smaller than the body of the hat, so it fit snugly over the ears.

Socks

For any sock pattern: After casting on, do one knit row (even if the pattern is cable or ribbing) to "even up the setup and absorb any unevenness. The eye won't notice it, and the finished product will look good."

Hats and Mittens

Ann was firm: "To be warm, they must be wool. Acrylic is not warm."

Baby Blankets

No fringes! The child will chew them and pull them off!
Make it reversible: The mother can grab the blanket and go, and it always looks good.

Use light yarn for the baby's comfort (Ann admonished against the too-common tendency of overbundling infants). Use worsted weight if you want to use the blanket as a floor play area.

Decorative Trims, Fringes, and Edges

Ann collected patterns for fancy knitted edges: knit tassles, balls, corkscrews, etc. For baby blankets, she especially liked sawtooth edge, a sturdy, unisex edging (patterns are readily available on the Internet). A decorative knit edge gives a lot of bang for the buck, and is an easy way to add pizzazz to your project.

Afghans

Making a large afghan can be daunting. Instead, try a patchwork afghan with 8-9-inch squares. It is a good way to try different techniques, and handling small squares is terrifically convenient.

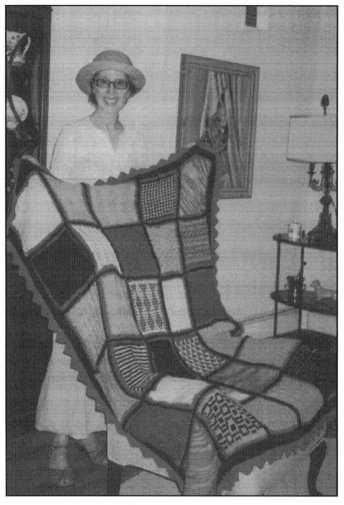

The author holds up her patchwork afghan.
The knitted squares are joined using crocheted stitches, and the border is knitted sawtooth edge.

ANN MADE DECISIONS that were ahead of her time. She was among the first American citizens to adopt a child from Brazil. Not only did she lead the way in adopting from a foreign country, she did so as a single parent. Ann was enormously proud of her daughter, Michelle, and spoke often and admiringly of her beauty and accomplishments.

Long before that, when Ann was a young teacher at John Adams High School at the height of the cold war, when air raids had students hiding from A-bombs under their desks, Ann decided it was time for a change of scenery. She got a job with the Department of Defense and was stationed at Camp Casey in South Korea, where she ran the Hourglass Service

Club as a Department of Defense civilian. At Camp Casey, Ann had a radio show, produced a James Brown concert, and coordinated recreational activities for the officers. She had the equivalent rank of major by the time she left.

Ann at her desk at the Hourglass Service Club, Camp Casey, South Korea

Director Action

Ann Sokolowski, program director of the Hourglass Service Club, unwinds a bit by doing the latest go-go dance during the 7th Inf. Div. Folk Rock Festival at Hanson Field House, Korea. About 1,500 people saw the one-performance-only festival, built around the "Joyful Noise" theme, including American girls, three rock bands, two folk bands and a jazz band. (USA)

Ann makes the news dancing at Camp Casey.

A stint in the military is a quite common way for a young man to get a job, leave home, and see the world; it is rather a more unusual choice for a woman. Ann was one of only 20 women among 15,000 men at her post.

In an article she penned describing the job, she sums up the experience: "Where else can you be paid to travel, meet fascinating people and live in new places?" On her vacation days, Ann managed to visit Hong Kong (twice), Bangkok, Japan, Singapore, Taiwan, Kuala Lumpur, Manila, and many other cities in Asia.

It must have been quite an adventure. Unfortunately, Ann suspected that this was the start of her physical troubles, due to an exposure to Agent Orange in Korea, which was commonly used as a pesticide in the area at that time.

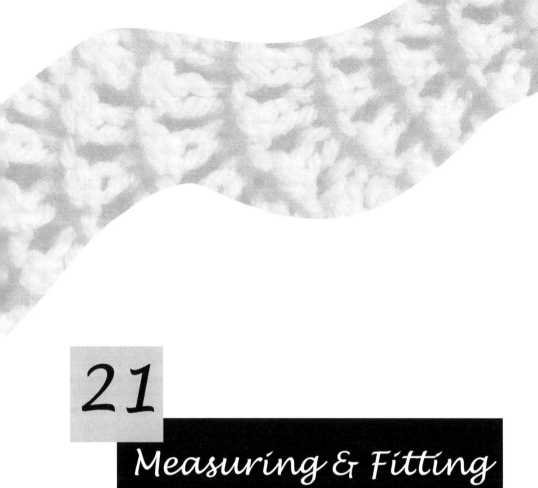

21

Measuring & Fitting

ANN OFFERED SKILLS rather than projects. Give a knitter a pattern and she can make a garment; give her the tools to make her own patterns and she is clothed for life. While most of us no longer need these skills in order to be clothed, the thrill in knowing how to do a thing from scratch is still immensely satisfying.

Ann obviously shared that thrill. Not only did she teach us how to measure and fit a variety of garments, in the ultimate salute to self-sufficiency she even taught us to measure sans measuring tools. Her students would be ready if we were stranded on a desert island without our tape measures!

Handy (Literally) Tools for Tape Measure-less Measuring

With one arm stretched straight out to the side, the distance between your nose and your outstretched fingertip is approximately one yard.

With your pointer finger stretched away from your thumb (as if shooting a pretend gun), the distance between the two fingers is approximately six inches.

Rule of thumb: The top joint of your thumb is approximately one inch.

Full body measure: Make a scarf as long as the wearer is tall. Hold up your favorite scarf and see. We did, and Ann's point held true.

Pinning as an Aid in Measuring for Sweaters

Ann was a big proponent of knitting sweaters from the neck down. (See the next chapter for her thoughts on the subject.) At our last class we were just beginning to delve into this fascinating area, and we were busy taking measurements for the project.

Before measuring, pin the following three points with big safety pins (Ann used quilter's pins). The pins function as stable reference points for the measurements. The person being measured should wear a garment that does not have too much play in it, or the measurements will not be reliable.

1. Shoulder:
Pin at the joint where the collarbone meets the top of the upper arm bone.

2. Neck:
Pin at the base of the neck, in the back.

3. Top of shoulder:
Pin along the flat of the shoulder, where you would place an epaulette.

Measuring for Sweaters

Once the person is pinned, take six measurements for Ann's sweater-knitted-from-the-neck-down project:

1. Neck to shoulder:
from the base of the side of the neck to the outer tip of the shoulder

2. Neck:
from one side of the base of the neck to the other side of the base of the neck (not the circumference of the neck)

3. Shoulder to shoulder:
from the outer tip of one shoulder (where the collarbone meets the upper arm bone) to the outer tip of the other shoulder

4. Shoulder to waist:
from the pin at the nape of neck to the waist

5. Shoulder to boobie (hey, this is Ann's book!):
from the pin on the flat of the shoulder to the widest part of the chest (usually at the nipple)

6. Shoulder to groin:
from the pin on the flat of the shoulder to the crease between the torso and leg

Sweater Measurements

A typical sweater is about 10 inches from top of shoulder to armpit and 17 inches from armpit to bottom of sweater, a total of 27 inches long.

Ann felt that for those under 5'6", a sweater is most flattering if it falls to the top of the hipbone; for those over 5'6", a sweater is most flattering if it falls to the crease where the torso meets the leg.

Hats

"You can't err too big. You can err too small." A roomy hat allows air to circulate, which helps insulate the head. A loose hat will be warmer than a tight hat.

Ann was amused by men's preference for a baggy top-space to a knitted cap, something to consider when knitting for a guy.

Caps with a cuff should be long enough for the cuff to roll down over the ears as needed. Add 3 inches for the cuff.

Women: head circumference 20-23 inches
Men: head circumference 22-24 inches
Children: too variable to generalize — take a measurement

(Circumference should be measured at the widest part of the head, at the eyebrows.)

Woman's hat: 10 inches long
Man's hat: 11-12 inches long
Child's hat: 8 inches long

Baby Blankets
36 x 36 inches makes a good carriage blanket.

36 x 42 inches makes a crib blanket that will be big enough when the child moves to a twin bed.

Know your own worth. Know what is worth your time and crafts-manship — and what is not.

ANN HAD A PRAGMATIC STREAK. She
thought a pattern for a newborn baby's cashmere bathrobe was the height of absurdity. "The kid will outgrow it in two minutes!"

Yet when I brought up the very practical idea of adding knit ribbed cuffs to a child's down jacket to keep it in use for another season, she explained how to accomplish it, but also advised against doing it. A hand-knit sweater, you see, is worth every effort to prolong its usefulness. It is an *heirloom*. On the other hand, a store-bought jacket, hand-knit cuffs notwithstanding, would always just be a store-bought jacket. A funky fix on a jacket would probably never really look right and, in Ann's view, did not merit the effort it would take to squeeze another year's use out of it.

To Ann, it was just plain common sense. But her common sense contained a deeper message: Know your own worth. Know what is worth your time and craftsmanship — and what is not.

129

22

Ann's Knit Projects

ANN LOVED KNITTING PATTERNS. She

collected them and was a fan of certain pattern writers. Yet while some people would be lost without a pattern, she believed that with a few guidelines her students should be able create their own patterns to suit their taste and needs.

Design choices were always in play: The Beginners Knit Sampler gave Ann's students a repertoire of skills at their command. From first to last, she demonstrated a genius for breaking down the elements of design and technique into flexible tools.

Ann's confidence in her students' intelligence and creativity has been empowering. In my life, knitting has become a source of great satisfaction. I use commercial patterns and make my own.

Ann's projects are a useful starting point for exploration. They are pattern *suggestions*, a road map highlighting points of interest to visit and pitfalls to avoid.

Ann's All-Purpose Hat Pattern

This hat features a two-stitch-wide rib stitch. Incredibly, the hat I made fit both adults and children: The ribs expand or shrink as needed, no matter the size of the wearer's head.

The project offers good practice calculating the number of stitches to cast on. The hat knits from the bottom up, so the cast on stitches need to fit the circumference of the head.

Just multiply the circumference of the wearer's head by the gauge. For example: A 22-inch-circumference head × 5 stitches/inch (worsted-weight gauge) = 110 stitches needed to cast on.

This rib is a four-stitch repeat (K2, P2), so best to cast on in multiples of four. Because 110 is not a number evenly divisible by four, adjust up or down — your choice — and cast on 112 or 108 stitches.

After determining the number of stitches to cast on, add two more stitches for edging (per Ann's rule of good edges). Your total will be either 114 or 110 stitches (after all!).

She believed that with a few guidelines her students should be able create their own patterns to suit their taste and needs.

A variant on Ann's Simple Hat Pattern is a one-stitch-wide rib (K1, P1), some-times called a Night Watchman Cap. Cast on in multiples of two — easy!

To make the body of the hat, rib stitch to the desired length. Ann offered three options for finishing the hat:

Finish the Hat Option A: No Decreases
Run your end tail (which you kept nice and long) through all the top stitches with a needlepoint needle and pull it tight (i.e., gather the top). No need to cast off: Simply thread the loops and gather them to form the top of the hat.

Overcast two or three times to secure the gather. Turn the hat inside out and continue sewing down the length of the hat (the side seam). Bury any re-maining tail.

Finish the Hat Option B: Decrease Gradually
At 9 or 10 inches, decrease on both ends of your row every four stitches. As Ann picturesquely put it, "Keep going as you wish, or at some point just put it out of its misery and gather it up," as per Option A, above. Use the tail to sew the hat, as in Option A.

Finish the Hat Option C: Decrease Rapidly
At 10 or 11 inches, decrease every other stitch (at this point you will drop your rib pattern). Keep going until you cannot decrease anymore, or at some point, again, just "put it out of its misery and gather it up," using the tail to sew the hat, as in Option A.

Ann's Go-To Basketweave Scarf
This scarf uses about three balls of yarn. Ann recommended using single-color yarn so the pattern is visible.

One-inch-wide squares are the simplest option. Multiply as many inches as you need by five stitches per inch (worsted weight yarn), and that is your basic stitch count. Per Ann's "Eye Happy, I Happy" design tip, use an odd num-ber of squares.

Add three non-curling edge stitches on both sides to help the scarf lay flat. Garter stitch or moss stitch serve well.

Finally, add two more stitches for Ann's usual Rule of Good Edges slip-the-first-stitch-and-knit-the-last-stitch addition to the pattern.

Here are sample calculations for a scarf that will be just over six inches wide:

    5 x 5-stitch basketweave squares = 25
    2 x 3-stitch non-curling edges = 6
    2 edge stitches = 2
    Total # stitches to cast on = 33

Ann's Go-To Basketweave Scarf Pattern

This scarf uses garter stitch as the non-rolling edge. To keep things simple, this pattern makes each square five rows high.

Cast on 33 stitches.

Rows 1, 3, 5, 6, 8, 10: Slip 1, K8, P5, K5, P5, K5, K4
Rows 2, 4, 7, 9: Slip1, K3, P5, K5, P5, K5, P5, K4

Repeat Rows 1-10 to the desired length.

Ann's Baby Blanket Knit on the Diagonal

Diagonal stockinette stitch creates the element of visual interest. Use self-striping yarn (yarn with multiple colors or shades dyed in various lengths or segments) to highlight the diagonal feature.

Cast on three or five stitches.

All right-side rows: Use all knit (and knit-wise) stitches. Increase by two stitches every right-side row, one increase at the beginning and one increase at the end of the row. (You will be knitting a triangle. As the blanket grows you will have ever more stitches in between the two increases.) (When you have enough stitches on your needle, do your increases one stitch in from the edge, not on the edge.)

All wrong-side rows: Purl across to end of row. No increases.

At the desired width: To transition, do two rows on pattern (all knit, all purl), with no increasing or decreasing.

All right side rows: Use all knit (and knit-wise) stitches. Decrease by two stitches every right-side row, one decrease at each end of the row. (Ann's tip: decrease one stitch in from the edge to make an even edge.)

135

All wrong side rows: Purl across to end of row. No decreases.

Bind off when you get down to the same number of stitches as you originally cast on (i.e., three or five stitches).

Squares knit on the diagonal tend to pull a little to one side, so your blanket may need blocking to get the square true to form. Stockinette stitch tends to curl, so you may want to add a crochet or knit border to help the blanket lay flat.

Easier Option for Ann's Baby Blanket on the Diagonal
Do the increases and decreases only at the start of every row, on both the right and wrong sides (rather than at the start and end of the right side rows). This allows you to zip to the end of each row without thinking.

Easiest Option for Ann's Baby Blanket on the Diagonal
As above, do all your increases and decreases at the start of every row. Knit the whole darn thing in garter stitch. No more right side or wrong side. Just knit, knit, knit.

This almost merits the title: "Ann's Great Mindless Baby Blanket Project." Almost. The next blanket wins the contest.

Ann's Great Mindless Baby Blanket Project (Ann's Title)
Ann liked the occasional mindless project where she could go on automatic as she knit. She even spoke about being able to knit without looking at what she was doing — while watching a movie, for example. (Of course, I had to try it the minute I heard about it. Suffice to say I was not quite ready for knitting blind.)

Again, use self-striping yarn for visual interest. Decide on the size you want to make your blanket and cast on accordingly (e.g., 36 inches × 5 stitches per inch = 180 stitches). Garter stitch the whole darn thing. Is that easy, or what?

Add a Border
Assuming you have had enough of a mental vacation, Ann suggested adding a border around the blanket to spike up the visual interest.

Crocheted edges are varied and lovely. Ann only cautioned against lacey designs or fringes that may choke the baby or tangle fingers.

One of her favorite knit edges was sawtooth edge. It is unisex, fun, and sturdy.

For something fancier, Ann thought a cabled border would set off a blanket like an ornate frame around a painting.

Ann's Baby Blanket for Her New Nephew

During the course of our classes, Ann was working on a baby blanket for her new grand nephew. I thought it might be interesting to recount some of what she shared about the project.

While Ann had a starting concept, she also modified the design as she went along. It was a garter-stitch blanket with a basketweave border. The original design included a basketweave medallion in the center, worked in the same wool as the body of the blanket. It eventually became a multi-colored intarsia medallion.

The blanket was made of worsted-weight Canadiana 100 percent acrylic yarn, chosen for its quality, heft, and wash-ability. Ann wanted the blanket to be large enough to use as a floor play area. Garter stitch provided thickness that made it comfortable for a baby to lie or crawl on.

The blanket was 36-inch square. Ann wanted it big enough to tuck around the baby in a carriage. The pattern was fully reversible. The baby's mother wouldn't have to worry about which side was up, she could just "throw it on and go!"

The main color was peacock blue, and the center medallion consisted of nine checkerboard squares in navy and red. The medallion was intended not just to look pretty, but also to attract the baby's eye; when the blanket was used on the floor, hopefully the multi-colored medallion would help keep the baby from crawling off. (We can try, right?)

To calculate the placement of the medallion, Ann used quilter's pins to mark off distances from the inside edges of the borders and from the center, so she would know where in the row to start her medallion. She also used her basketweave border (an odd number of squares in sets of five stitches each) at the bottom of the blanket to count out from the center, using quilter's pins as markers, and moving up to the middle of the blanket from there in order to map out her medallion.

"Do it right and wear it with pride!" Plan and revise, check and recheck your plans and your progress as you proceed.

Take the time to use the pins as an aid in marking off distances, and calculate your

> *Ann trusted her own intelligence and ability. How rare it is to be able to say that about someone!*

plan from different angles (does the medallion grow out from the center symmetrically? Are the sides of the medallion equal distance from the borders?)

Mystifyingly, Michelle never found this project among her mother's belongings. Instead, she found the afghan squares, described in the section on Loose Ends, which we were privileged to assemble for her.

Catch the Kid: Ann's Child's Vest Pattern

Among my notes I found a handout of Ann's pattern for a child's knit vest. It exemplifies both her humor ("Catch the kid…") and her confident approach to pattern making.

I have a feeling that if someone came to Ann in a panic and told her that 20 unexpected guests were popping over for dinner that night, where others might suggest recipes, or hiring help, or going to a restaurant, Ann would say something like, "throw a few burgers on the grill, open a few beers, and you'll have a great party!" To some, winging it without an exact blueprint would be intimidating; Ann believed that anyone with a little intelligence should be able to pull it off.

Ann struck a winning balance. On the one hand, she kept the task in perspective — after all, she was writing about a child's vest, not rocket science — and as such, it did not merit panic, anxiety, or timidity. On the other hand, producing a nice knit garment is no mean feat — and as such it was fully worthy of a sense of pride, capability, and accomplishment.

Ann trusted her own intelligence and ability. How rare it is to be able to say that about someone! Her confidence was contagious, and it was a gift she shared freely with others. No wonder her high school students' grades soared when she taught them to knit.

Her full instructions are included here verbatim:

The neat thing about little kids is they're almost square. Their chests and waists and hips are all almost the same.

Catch the kid and measure the chest and shoulder to armpit and armpit to how long you want the vest to be. Now loop the measuring tape and get an idea on the neck.

For a pullover, take the chest measurement and add two or three inches for design ease. Multiply that number times the gauge for the yarn you want.

Cast on and join for circular knitting.

Work some rows of rib if you want or some rows of garter stitch to prevent curling.

Knit up to the underarm measurement (probably nine or ten inches).
Bind off one inch worth of stitches at the center of each underarm.

Back:
On the next four or six rows bind off (BO) two stitches at the beginning and end of each right-side row. Knit straight to shoulder (probably about five inches from underarm). Work two or three extra rows on shoulder stitches, reserving center six to seven inches for back of neck.

Front:
Work same as back, except put center four to five inches on holder or BO about one or one-and-a-half inches before shoulder. BO or hold in reserve two or three stitches every other row on each side of the neck opening until it matches back neck opening.

Finish shoulders.
BO or graft shoulder seams.

Pick up and knit a couple or three rows of rib or garter stitch around armholes and neck edge for trim or crochet a round or two.

Sweaters from the Neck Down
Ann was a big believer in knowing the terrain before embarking on a project. She was not going to have us make a sweater. Rather, we were to make a

sweater sampler, on which we would try out different types of collars, sleeves, and other techniques. From Ann's description, I imagine it as an octopus-like creature, fit for Halloween, or perhaps an avant-garde fashion runway.

An imagined Sweater from the Neck Down Sampler

Sweaters from the Neck Down Samplers Take Fashion World by Storm!

I hope Ann's enthusiasm for sweaters from the neck down will inspire further exploration of this subject. As a starting point, she recommended Ann Norling's raglan sweater patterns for adults and children.

Ann's Thoughts on Sweaters from the Neck Down

The entire project is knit on circular needles, working from the collar down. At the shoulders, where the sleeves branch off from the torso, the knitter chooses to work first on either the sleeves or the torso. The part that is not being worked is held on pause on stitch holders.

The way Ann saw it, making a sweater from the neck down offered several distinct advantages. For starters, the most complex part of the sweater was completed first (the collar, the set-in of the sleeves). Once over that major hump, just ease on through to the finish line, that is, knit down to the end of the sleeves and to the bottom of the garment.

A sweater from the neck down is worked as a unit. Ann contrasted this with the standard way of making a sweater in four big pieces — front, back, sleeve, and sleeve — which can feel like four separate large knit projects (or five, for a cardigan, or more if there is an added collar). And then you still have to sew it together! Will it ever get done?

Both sleeves are knit at the same time, knitting left and right arms side by side, row for row. This helps the sleeves come out evenly in relation to each other. (This is not exclusive to sweaters from the neck down; sleeves can be knit side by side on any sweater project, except when the sleeves are done in a tubular fashion on circular needles.)

Knitting both sleeves at the same time, side by side and row for row, the gauge will be consistent. In contrast, doing the sleeves separately, sometimes putting the project aside for an extended period of time, it is hit or miss to match the gauges of the two sleeves. Even counting rows, chances are the two sleeves will not match.

The sleeves are not worked circularly. You can use circular needles, but each sleeve is flat, not tubular. You will need to sew the sleeve seams. Ann recommended starting at the cuff, and working your way up to the armpit to help line the seam up more easily.

The torso is knit in a circle; there are no side seams. This is labor saving, avoids the dreaded bulky side seam, and leaves that much less room for error.

A final benefit to this technique comes into play when making a child's sweater. Ann often quoted her mother: "Children grow up, not out!" As mentioned,

Ann recommended making a child's sweater without any cuffs or bottom rib-bing. As the child grows, simply add 3-4 inches of cuffs and ribbing and get another few years of wear out of the sweater. Because the sweater from the neck down ends at the bottom of the garment, it is particularly convenient to simply undo the cast off edge, pick up the loops, and continue knitting. Your cuffs and ribbing will be integral to the garment.

Again, this can be taken to extremes . . .

A present from Grandma

23

The End of Yarn

I WILL ALWAYS BE INDEBTED to Ann for entrusting me with her teachings and her story, for inspiring me with the confidence to follow the voice in my head in completely unexpected directions, and for awakening my love of knitting and the friendships and joys it contains. As my knitting world continues to expand I have connected with knitters on the Internet, among friends, and in my family. Pulling out a pair of needles on a New York City subway has been like a beacon to other knitters; I've struck up conversations and friendships with people from all over the world. What an awesome community!

a quietly extra-ordinary individual

I am deeply grateful for the opportunity to put this experience to paper. I hope I have succeeded in conveying some of Ann's wit and personality. Not least, I feel compelled to share what I know of Ann's story, and to honor her both as a unique teacher and as a quietly extraordinary individual.

At first I did not understand what compelled me to write about her; the pattern of the design only became clear as I wrote. I marvel at the symmetry of a universe in which Ann provided such a precise answer to my personal trauma: Where my struggle had been with fine appearances masking inner callousness, Ann presented a tough-guy exterior cloaking the purest generosity, faith, and caring; where I had felt cut out from the narrative of my parents' lives, Ann bequeathed me her story; where I had felt silenced, Ann gave me an opening to speak. Who would have guessed that such a profound healing would be delivered in the form of a wise-cracking knitting teacher at the Y? Slowly, the threads that knit our stories together became apparent, and the gems of wisdom embedded in the experience were revealed. I will remember Ann with gratitude, always.

Where there are gaps in my notes from Ann's classes I have not tried to fill in the missing pieces, nor have I attempted to present myself as an authority on all things knitted. Incomplete though some of the information may be, I believe that what we received from Ann was uniquely useful and worthy of being passed along.

Ann pointed the way to fill in any gaps in information. She encouraged us to visit online tutorials, get the best books, and *keep learning*. I would like to add to Ann's recommendations my own encouragement to get together with others. Learn together and learn from one another. If it does not feel right, walk away. May you be fortunate enough to find a teacher who makes your heart sing.

Do this old-fashioned art the old-fashioned way — with the human touch — and make discoveries about product and process that may well serve to mend the gaps in our busy, electronic world. In doing so, you will be carrying on the tradition that Ann herself honored when she volunteered to teach at the Y and shared herself so fully with her class.

May your knitting bring you joy.

Appendix A

Photo Album

Ann as a baby in 1941 with her mother,
Stella Sokolowski —
note the hand-crocheted baby outfit.

First communion, May 1950

School portrait,
probably around age nine

Eighth grade graduation, 1955

John Adams High School Graduation Day, June 1959

Happy Holidays!

Ann with her parents, Stella and Stanley Sokolowski

At a recreation center party at Camp Casey, South Korea

At the Hourglass Service Club, Camp Casey, South Korea

Ann with an unidentified soldier at Camp Casey,
holding an "automatic blanket," i.e., an electric blanket

151

An ecstatic new mom
with her daughter, Michelle

With her Scottish Terrier, Fiona

I snapped this cell phone shot of Ann a few months after we met.
This was the Ann that I knew.

Appendix B

Ann's Favorite Fancy Stitch Variations

Here are some of Ann's favorite stitch variations, as she gave them to us. Some topics are more detailed than others.

Pick and choose what interests you. My view is that Ann's genius lay not so much in her instructions, but more specifically in her approach to learning and creating, as well as in her insights into technique.

Ann had us make mini-samplers for cables, basketweave, intarsia, feather and fan, and others. They were not formal samplers. We did just enough to get the idea of how the stitch worked in practice. I am sure she would encourage you to do the same.

BASKETWEAVE

Basketweave is a checkerboard pattern alternating knit and purl boxes, more precisely, alternating stockinette and reverse stockinette squares. It was the first stitch we learned after we finished our Beginner Knit Sampler.

Basketweave is reversible and lies flat. It is a simple pattern that offers myriad ways to make a personal statement by varying the size and texture of the squares. It is geometric and effective in both men's and women's garments.

Ann used basketweave as a teaching tool. The pattern offers rigorous training in doing and not doing what presents. It also provides a manageable canvas on which to explore a variety of options. Ann had us learn basics of lace, texture, and color through variations on basketweave.

Ann's fundamental basketweave pattern uses squares five stitches wide and five stitches high. As per her rule of symmetry, she used an *odd* number of multiples (i.e., five sets of five = 25 stitches).

The pattern below works only with an odd number of squares. (Basketweave may be done with an even number of squares, but the pattern will be different.)

BASKETWEAVE

Cast on in multiples of 5 stitches.

Rows 1, 3, 5, 6, 8, 10: *K5, P5, repeat from * across row, when 5 stitches remain, then K5
Rows 2, 4, 7, 9: *P5, K5, repeat from * across row, when 5 stitches remain, then P5

Repeat Rows 1-10 to the desired length.

Basketweave

Note the checkerboard pattern. A variant of the stitch, also called basketweave, gives an interlocking effect, like the interwoven slats of a basket. Barbara Walker offers that variation in her *Learn to Knit Afghan Book.*

BASKETWEAVE: MOSS STITCH SQUARES

Ann got creative by varying the texture of individual squares. She suggested replacing some or all of the purl squares with moss stitch.

MOSS STITCH SQUARE

Within one purl-side-forward 5-stitch square, instead of five rows of reverse stockinette, do:

Rows 1-5: P1, K1, P1, K1, P1

Basketweave with moss stitch squares

Ann also experimented with replacing some or all of the knit squares with alternating rows of moss and knit stitches.

MOSS STITCH SQUARE VARIATION 1

Within one knit-side-forward 5-stitch square, instead of five rows of stockinette, do:

Rows 1, 3, 5: K1, P1, K1, P1, K1
Rows 2, 4: Purl across

Basketweave with moss stitch variation 1, wrong side

MOSS STITCH SQUARE VARIATION 2

Within one knit-side-forward 5-stitch square, instead of five rows of stockinette, do:

Rows 1, 3, 5: Knit across
Rows 2, 4: K1, P1, K1, P1, K1

Basketweave square with moss stitch variation 2

BASKETWEAVE: DROPPED STITCH LACEY EFFECT

Ann liked a lacey effect created by deliberately dropping stitches. The dropped stitches make a vertical ladder, like a run in a stocking. As with all lace work, in order to maintain the total number of stitches, a stitch is added for every stitch that is dropped.

In a basketweave square that is five stitches across, drop one, two, or three stitches. Ann's only caveat was to drop no more than three stitches per square, or there won't be enough substance to frame the dropped stitches.

The sample pattern supposes a basketweave square that is five stitches wide and five stitches high.

BASKETWEAVE DROPPED STITCH

In one knit-side-forward 5-stitch square, instead do:

Row 1: *K1, M1, K1, M1, K1
Rows 2, 4: *P7
Rows 3, 5: *K7
Row 6: K2, D1, K1, D1, K2

M1 = Make one stitch (increase 1)
D1 = Drop one stitch

After you complete row 6, give the garment a horizontal tug: The dropped stitches will run down to point of pick up.

Basketweave with dropped stitches in the knit squares
(the dropped stitches do not read as well as they might in a bigger square)

Basketweave with dropped stitches, wrong side
(the dropped stitches create an interesting puffiness on this side)

Ann suggested dropping a stitch(es) in every square that would have been a knit square, or in selected squares to create a pattern of lacey squares within the whole.

BASKETWEAVE: INCREASE/DECREASE LACEY EFFECT

Ann suggested increasing and decreasing within a square — a simple introduction to the world of knit lace. Though we did not practice this stitch in class, we grasped the concept and understood that most lace patterns would be variations on this theme.

Like most lace work, Ann's variations use yarn overs (YO) as the increase of choice to create a lacey hole in the fabric.

She gave us two decreasing methods: *knit two together* (K2TOG) and *pass the slip stitch over* (PSSO). Both are effective, but different, so Ann advised to choose one and stick with it.

Following are two options for a five-stitch-across basketweave square.

BASKETWEAVE INCREASE/DECREASE VARIATION I

On a knit-side-forward 5-stitch square, instead do:

Rows 1, 3, 5: Knit across
Rows 2, 4: P2TOG, YU, P1, YU, P2TOG

Or, on a purl-side-forward 5-stitch square, instead do:

Rows 1, 3, 5: Purl across
Rows 2, 4: K2TOG, YO, K1, YO, K2TOG

Basketweave Increase/Decrease Variation 1

Basketweave Increase/Decrease Variation 1, reverse side

BASKETWEAVE INCREASE/DECREASE VARIATION 2
On a knit-side-forward 5-stitch square, instead do:

Rows 1, 3, 5: PSSO, YO, K1, YO, PSSO
Rows 2, 4: Purl across

Or, on a purl-side-forward 5-stitch square, instead do:

Rows 1, 3, 5: PSSO (purl-wise), YU, P1, YU, PSSO (purl-wise)
Rows 2, 4: Knit across

Each increase/decrease combination equals one regular knit stitch. As usual, lacey rows alternate with purl across or knit across rows in order to stabilize the fabric.

INTARSIA BASKETWEAVE SQUARES
Intarsia creates blocks of color in patterns as simple as a square patch or as complex as an impressionistic garden. Once again, Ann used the ever-useful basketweave to introduce a new technique in a manageable form. It was a happy choice not only for teaching purposes: The intarsia basketweave squares are an eye-catching aesthetic fit as well, with color squares highlighting the graphic checkerboard pattern.

Each square gets its own precut length of yarn, which gets used up row by row. In the midst of an intarsia project, typically there will be multiple balls of yarn hanging from the project. Roll the dangling yarns into mini-balls, or bobbin them up with any type of clip.

ANN'S SUPER-EASY INTARSIA INSTRUCTIONS
Every square has its own yarn. Ann's instructions were to the point: Knit your five stitches in Color A, then set down the Color A yarn (it will be dangling from your knitting) and start on Color B.

When changing colors, the new color must come from underneath the old color, otherwise there will be a hole in between the two colors. Laying the new yarn under the old (crossing the old yarn over the new is another way to express it) twists the two yarns together, and that twist knits the two colors together without a gap in between.

Ann's instructions were that simple. And, by gosh, they worked.

PRE-MEASURE YARN FOR INTARSIA SQUARES
If you ever venture into intarsia territory, Ann's tip is a keeper: Pre-measure the yarn. No more guesswork, and no more wasted yarn or effort.

For example, to find the length of yarn needed for each intarsia square in the basketweave variation, make a sample square the same size as the intarsia squares. If your squares are five stitches across and five rows high, cast on five stitches and knit a sample square five rows up.

Snip your yarn, leaving a six-inch or so tail at both start and finish.

Now, unravel your sample square. Yes, undo all your good work. Once you have done that, simply measure the length of the yarn your sample square used. Now you know how much each square will use and you can pre-cut your yarn lengths in the colors as needed.

Always add a few extra inches for good measure when you pre-cut your yarn. Bundle the yarns into mini-balls (see chapter on Balls and Skeins) and you are ready to start your intarsia project.

Genius!

FAIR ISLE KNITS

Fair Isle knitting features multiple rows of patterned design in varying colors. The technique involves knitting with multiple strands of yarn, carrying unused threads behind the garment, on the wrong side.

Ann's tip: Every inch, anchor the yarn being carried across the wrong side. Just twist it around the yarn you are knitting with and carry on with your pattern. In effect, you are tacking the yarn to the back of the fabric.

In terms of Fair Isle design, Ann knew that too many bright colors would compete against each other and cancel out their effectiveness. Her strategy urged using a spectrum of dull colors, set off by one acid bright color that would pop and enliven the whole design.

MOSAIC KNITS

Mosaic is worked in two colors using slip stitches to create complex patterns. Color A is knitted across and back, then Color B is picked up and knitted across and back, alternating up the fabric.

The slip stitches in mosaic knits are essentially elongated stitches, carried up from one row to the next. Pulling the stitch from one row to the next, plus the yarn that runs behind the slip stitches, gives an extra thickness to mosaic fabric, making for really toasty knitwear. Surely, the technique was developed in cold climes.

CABLE PATTERNS

Cable patterns typically look like twists of rope, braids, or other designs that move across the fabric. They have such a bold effect that they may seem daunting. Nonetheless, they are quite simple to do.

Cables are accomplished by holding a small number of stitches aside while you knit other stitches, then pulling those set-aside stitches across and knitting them into the fabric.

A simple cable, surrounded and offset by a garter stitch background

SAMPLE CABLE PATTERN

Make each strand of the cable four stitches wide, eight stitches total for the two strands. Add four additional stitches on each side to offset the cable: Cast on 16 stitches.

The surrounding or background stitches (four on each side, in Ann's example) should be reverse stockinette, seed, or garter stitched to frame out the cable. As Ann would say: "You need the framing in order to see the work." The cable itself uses stockinette. This visually brings the cable forward to stand out in relief against the background stitches.

Do the four background stitches, then knit Strand A and Strand B of the cable (knit eight stitches). Work back and forth a few rows (say, four, for example) until you are ready to make the twist of the cable.

To make the twist in the cable, knit the four background stitches, then slip the first four stitches of the cable — Strand A — onto a cable holder. Allow the cable holder with the four stitches on it to just hang (front or back) while you proceed to knit the four stitches of Strand B.

Next, pick up the cable holder and knit Strand A off the cable holder and onto the regular needles. To do this, you will be pulling Strand A across Strand B in order to knit it. That makes the twist. Just pull it across. It may seem awkward and a bit tight at first, but as you keep going, the cable takes shape.

Once you have made the twist, knit up four or more rows before you cross over again to give some height to the cables and some ease to the fabric.

That's all there is to it. Use a cable holder that is thinner than your knitting needles so as not to overstretch your stitches.

CABLE VARIATIONS

Play with the length of the cables — short twists and bulky yarns make the traditional fisherman's sweater, and elongated cables and fine yarns create the elegant lines of the classic tennis sweater. If Strand A hangs in front of your knitting, it creates a left twist; if it hangs behind your knitting, it makes a right twist. Twists can cross and uncross, creating threading, winding, ribbon-like effects. Some cable patterns are as complex as Celtic knots, testaments to the creative genius of the women who made them.

SAWTOOTH EDGE

Ann liked that sawtooth edge can be integral to the body of the work, that is, it is knit directly on to the body of the piece, rather than sewn on. Nonetheless, if you prefer, or don't want to travel with a whole project in tow, you can make the edge separately, then sew it on.

Ann did not give us a sawtooth edge pattern, but she spoke of it many times. I found a pattern on the Internet (there are many available) and used it on my afghan (see a photo of the afghan on page 122).

FEATHER AND FAN

Ann knew this 18-stitch-repeat pattern as Feather and Fan. It should be noted that some folks recognize this stitch as Old Shale, and reserve the name Feather and Fan for a similar 14-stitch-repeat pattern. For the purposes of this book, we are sticking with Ann's terminology. Feather and fan is easy and it makes a very distinctive pattern. It is somewhat lacey and works well for scarves and shawls.

Because the pattern repeat is 18 stitches long, use stitch markers in between each repeat. In fact, stitch markers were part of the pattern as Ann gave it to us.

FEATHER AND FAN
Cast on in multiples of 18 stitches.

Row 1: Knit across, placing stitch marker every 18 stitches
Row 2: Purl across
Row 3: *K2TOG 3XS, (YO, K1) 6XS, K2TOG 3XS, repeat from * to end of row
Row 4: Knit across

Repeat Rows 1-4 to the desired length.

The fabulous feather and fan stitch, bordered on both sides by garter stitch.
Note the lovely curved edge it creates.

Ann thought that feather and fan should be bordered on both outside edges by three or more garter stitches to stabilize the fabric (on both outer edges of the fabric). She felt it was effective to start and end your project with a few rows of garter stitch as well.

Feather and fan is directional. The pattern, when repeated, creates a scallop-y wave and the fans all face one way; they have a top and a bottom. This does not bother some folks (myself included).

However, it should be noted that to make a truly symmetrical scarf or shawl, the pattern should start in the middle and work outward in two directions, or start from both ends and work inward toward the middle. Because that essentially means creating the cloth out of two pieces, it will take some skilled joining to execute either option unobtrusively. You might want to learn more about grafting, a subject Ann only touched on briefly (see page 100).

Made in the USA
Lexington, KY
20 July 2014